ELBOW
ROOM

A Tale of Tenacity on Kodiak Island, Alaska

ELBOW ROOM

A TALE OF TENACITY ON KODIAK ISLAND, ALASKA

D. D. FISHER

Aventine Press

Published by Aventine Press
55 E Emerson Street
Chula Vista, CA 91911

ISBN: 1-59330-749-7

Library of Congress Control Number: 2011919380

Printed in the United States of America

Dedicated to Greg,
who taught me well.

ACKNOWLEDGEMENTS

My deepest gratitude to my husband and lifetime partner for his support and encouragement during the long months I worked on this project. Grateful thanks to my sister, Debbie, for reading my early and very rough drafts, and long-distance encouragement to "keep it up." My heartfelt thanks to the numerous friends in Kodiak whose kindness and help made our life on the rock so enjoyable.

AUTHOR'S NOTE

Located in the Gulf of Alaska, Kodiak Island is the largest in the state, measuring 3,588 square miles and accessible only by a one-hour plane ride or a twelve-hour ferry ride from the mainland. We moved to Kodiak site unseen and found a unique blend of beauty and bitterness, richness and depravity, wildness and serenity.

In the 1980s, there were no shopping malls, half the residents still didn't have running water, electricity was intermittent with frequent brown outs and luxury items were anything that couldn't be handcrafted or borrowed from a friend. The climate was harsh with cold snowy blizzards that blasted through long dark winters followed by wet, foggy, springs and damp rainy summers. The small fishing village was ten years behind the times in technology, engineering and even some basic modern amenities.

Still, we became mesmerized by the abundant wildlife, sea life, and a strange but innovative lifestyle that depended on tides and winds and the pristine but dangerous environment. Somewhere along the way, we got caught up in the battle of man against Mother Nature. Each small victory fueled our determination to face the next challenge, as each major setback brought us closer to the truth.

We stayed on this remote island for more than twenty-five years and felt privileged to share the lives of people who faced the daily challenges of this mostly uninhabited and harsh land. These determined individuals struggled and strived to maintain a lifestyle unlike any other, and so reaped the benefits of Elbow Room.

This is a work of creative nonfiction based on my own experiences, opinions, and imagination. Some details were altered and names were changed to protect the privacy of individuals.

CONTENTS

CHAPTER 1 ARRIVAL   1
CHAPTER 2 CRABBY   7
CHAPTER 3 JUST PLAIN LUCKY   15
CHAPTER 4 CLOSE NEIGHBORS   31
CHAPTER 5 WAITING   37
CHAPTER 6 STELLAR PERFORMANCE   39
CHAPTER 7 DELUGE   49
CHAPTER 8 CHECKMATES   59
CHAPTER 9 THE CHALLENGE   75
CHAPTER 10 RURAL AWAKENING   81
CHAPTER 11 LAST HAUL   97
CHAPTER 12 OPPORTUNISTS   101
CHAPTER 13 ON BUILDING A HOUSE   109
CHAPTER 14 THE YEAR OF THE BEAR   119
CHAPTER 15 VISITORS   123
CHAPTER 16 RUNNING WITH BEARS   137
CHAPTER 17 IT'S A DOG'S TOWN   141
CHAPTER 18 TREE SMART   149
CHAPTER 19 CABIN CACHE   157
CHAPTER 20 LIKE DUCKS ON WATER   163
CHAPTER 21 FISHING FOR BEAR   171
CHAPTER 22 DEPARTING   177

1 ARRIVAL

B eing upbeat and positive, while useful in sorting out certain situations, was not always easy, and being upbeat and positive while bumping around at 30,000 feet in a compact aircraft designed to haul freight was downright difficult. I gripped both armrests tightly and pressed my feet to the floor as the cramped, stuffy plane banked hard to the right.

The wide span of flat metal wings tipped almost vertical as we circled around lush green mountains that were still wearing white snowcaps with white ribbons streaming down the crevices of the high rocky peaks. The plane suddenly dropped altitude and the nose shot down towards the ocean. I hoped this was it.

George and I had moved seven times in the first ten years of our marriage, partly because of a restlessness acquired from the obligatory military moves during George's hitch with the Air Force, and partly because of an inner quest of George's to "find our niche." I tagged along each time, learning to pack and unpack with surprising efficiency, and typically felt that each new start brought new hope.

But this place was remote. We had always lived in big cities. Kodiak Island was not even on most maps of the United States.

The few that depicted the Great Land showed Kodiak to be a smudge just below the left leg that swung out into the Pacific Ocean like some artist's mistake.

"It'll be great, you'll see," said George when I pointed out that the nearest mainland was two hundred fifty miles by air or twelve hours by a large four hundred foot ferry, according to a *Milepost* discovered in the local Colorado Springs library. The dusty dog-eared travel guide contained descriptions of Alaskan cities, towns, and other places of interest, including road maps and populations, but little was mentioned about Kodiak. The Internet would have been useful back then.

Kodiak was a small island in the middle of the Gulf of Alaska with no road access, no big city close by, and nobody we knew had ever heard of it.

"It's still part of America," persuaded George, "and people do live there. See, the description says population 6,195 and look, there's even a college."

"But it's *Alaska*, George. It's cold in Alaska. So cold that Eskimos live in igloos and all the animals are white because of all the white snow. And that figure probably includes dogs, cats, *and* bears. And they say it's really dark up there, too," I protested.

No argument reached his adventurous self. George was always determined to see what was over the horizon, always ready for the next adventure. He clung to his belief that something better was always around the corner. I clung to the last few personal treasures that I knew I would have to leave behind.

It was April 1984 when George packed up his 1973 Chevy pickup and departed for Kodiak. I sold our house in Colorado three months later and loaded Blackie, our two- year-old black Labrador, into my compact car and hit the road. We reached Seattle in four long, bleary-eyed days, stopping along the way for brief rests and drive-up meals. From there the dog and I flew to Anchorage, and then took another one-hour flight out into the

Gulf of Alaska to the remote island of Kodiak. The car arrived three weeks later by barge.

The airplane suddenly leveled off, gliding just feet above crystal blue water rumpled and dimpled in its age-old effort to keep in rhythm with the ebbs and flows of the ocean tides. White dashes of foamy waves appeared and disappeared from the watery depths below. A miniature silver and blue boat grew larger and larger, and then rushed by the rounded porthole window of the plane. I could see the beginning of the runway sticking out over the ocean like a flat gray tongue sticking out of the face of the mountain that stood like a granite wall dead ahead.

I heard the landing gear groan down in place and felt the hard bump as the wheels nicked the surface once before skidding down on the tongue. The afterburners roared up loud and the passengers leaned forward in unison as the aircraft suddenly braked to a crawl and the pilot steered the plane across the tarmac and then around in a full circle to face the ocean again.

It was a sunny August morning when we pulled to a full stop in front of a small metal building labeled Kodiak Airport. No gangway tunnel pushed out to greet the plane; instead, a rack of stairs wheeled over by the ground crew was clipped to the door.

When the door hatch swung out and up, I gingerly climbed down the ladder in single file with the other passengers, glancing quickly around. The breeze was cool on my face, the air smelled clean and salty. A sort of tangy weedy scent brushed past me as I caught glimpses of green trees and green bushes and green grass. No tall buildings. Not one skyscraper stood in the distance. Just trees, grass, and water everywhere. I continued in line, pulling my carry-on behind me and into the terminal, a building about the size of a two-car garage located seventy-five feet from the plane.

The checked luggage suddenly appeared, one by one, through a plastic-covered opening, and rolled around a small carousel only to disappear again. I quickly snatched my black bag on the second go-around. The other wall held three ticket

counters shared by Wein and Pen Air, the only two airlines that
served Kodiak. The third wall included the entrance doors, two
rental car agents and two restrooms. The fourth wall held a few
rows of chairs occupied by those waiting to depart on the same
plane. I collected my luggage, walked the thirty feet to the exit
doors, and met George coming in.

"Hey, George," I said, reaching for a hug.

"You made it. Welcome to Kodiak," said George. He wore
a wide grin and pulled me to him, his sky blue eyes bright and
shining. His straight blond hair, mostly hidden under a Steelers
ball cap, edged over his ears and down his neck to the collar
of his red fleece-lined flannel shirt. His matching mustache was
neatly trimmed over thin lips and a curly blond beard circled his
chin and cheeks, meeting up with longish sideburns framing a
pleasing, friendly face.

I followed George over to the cargo entrance of the hangar
to pick up Blackie. George carried the dog crate out to a grassy
area and opened the kennel. Blackie leaped up and into George's
face with sloppy doggy kisses, then scampered over to the nearest alder bush to do his business. With furious tail wagging and
nose snuffling, he was eagerly taking it all in. He seemed a lot
more enthusiastic about being here than I did.

Blackie stopped short, turned and bounded back to George,
who playfully tousled his ears and ruffled his smooth black fur,
delighted to be with his beloved companion after the long separa-
tion. I looked on at the happy scene then my eyes shifted around,
taking in this strange green wilderness. Cars were quickly leaving the parking lot and only a handful of people loitered about. I
fought back the urge to get on the plane and fly back to civiliza-
tion. But I hated flying.

We walked to the truck, tossed the luggage and dog crate in
the back, then the three of us climbed in front and headed out of
the parking lot. George turned right, and then took an immediate
left heading down a two-lane paved road for about a half mile.
The sign read "State Road Maintenance Ends" as we dropped

off the ledge of the pavement onto a bumpy potholed dirt road passing a bridge that crossed over the Buskin River. The bushy treed banks revealed glimpses of a fast-moving river about fifteen feet wide running parallel to the road.

After a quarter of a mile, we pulled over into a well-worn parking area and George turned off the truck.

"Let's go catch a fish." George said climbing out of the truck.

I missed a couple of beats as my eyebrows shot to the top of my head. "A fish? Now?"

"Yeah, come on. I caught one just before the plane landed. We need to catch one more for dinner tonight," George announced.

I was dressed in my favorite brown velvet pantsuit with a white silk blouse and matching brown leather pumps. My long brown hair was neatly braided and twisted into a knot on the back of my head for ease of travel, and to ensure I arrived looking my best. Reluctantly, I got out of the truck, toe stepping over puddles and around patches of dark red gunky stains topped with pale fish skeletons of various sizes scattered over the muddy grass.

I reached the other side of the truck and stood watching as George eagerly raced across the road to the riverbank while pushing the two parts of his fishing rod together and clipping on an orange and silver striped lure.

He swung the rod back, jerked it forward, and the lure sailed across the river to just about a foot from the other side and landed with a neat splat. His fingers already working the reel, he glanced back at me and nodded me forward with his head. He turned quickly back and jerked hard one second after the rod tip bowed down, bending almost in half.

The rod continued jerking wildly up and down, the line peeled off the reel and a wave of water surged towards the far side. Several fins rose up out of the water, moving upstream like a herd of small sharks. One large silvery fish leaped into the air, turned his white belly up, twisted around and splashed back down, fighting hard to get free of the hook.

George hung onto the rod with both hands, struggling against the leaping fish. His eyes were wide, his jaw clenched and his arms were locked in place. A look of pure glee shown on his face as his feet stammered for a good hold on the sloping rocky riverbank, his hands frantically working the rod and reel, keeping pace with the huge fish.

"Get him," I shouted, "get him." I raced across the road and stood on the bank cheering him on. "Get him, Get him."

He landed the huge fish onto the bank, its slimy, silvery, scaly body flapping and flopping across my shoes. I jumped back but not before my brown velvet pant legs were spattered with salt water, slimy fish scales and mud up to my knees. I pasted a smile on my face before I looked up at George.

"Wow. This fish is huge!" I said. I was shocked. I had never seen such a big fish in my life. And my pantsuit was ruined. The fish lay there flat, thick, and finally dead on the muddy bank. George happily pulled out his knife and sliced the fish from tail to gills, cleaned it out, carried it over to the ice chest and plopped it in. I stared down at the catch of the day - large, shiny, and bloody. My airplane stomach lurched. *Dinner*?! I hefted a deep sigh and tried to stifle a shudder. I didn't know what to make of this place.

2 CRABBY

We rented an 850-square foot "cottage" for $850, which thankfully included electricity and home heating fuel - two of the high-cost commodities on the island. Kodiak did not have natural gas. Houses and commercial buildings used diesel fuel to operate boilers, forced-air furnaces or Toyo stoves. Most houses had woodstoves for supplemental heating in the winter, which worked well to stave off the moisture inside caused by the almost continuous rain and snow outside.

Tom was our neighbor, who introduced himself one day holding the largest king crab we had ever laid eyes on. George answered the quick two-rap on the door, pushed back the screen and there stood a solidly built man about five feet ten inches, with shaggy long brown hair, brown eyes, and a thick brown beard. He was dressed in a well-worn plaid flannel shirt and jeans that were wet from the thighs down to his brown rubber boots.

Tom held the crab by its two front legs with his arms stretched wide. The crab hung in a large V, its other four legs dangling down on both sides, almost reaching his knees.

"Hey Georgie." Tom's instantly chosen nickname stuck with George for many years to come. "Looky what I got." We stared at the spiky red and white blotchy creature as its viselike claws clipped menacingly at the air.

He stepped through the door and into the kitchen where he promptly slapped it down on the table, which was thankfully covered with a vinyl tablecloth. The crab sprawled across most of the five feet surface.

"What is it?" I gingerly asked, not bothering to mask my distaste as I backed away from the table.

"It's a king crab, silly. Haven't' you ever seen a king crab before?" I hadn't seen a king, queen or jack crab for that matter, and said as much.

"Wow," said Tom. "Where you guys from anyway?"

After brief introductions by way of a handshake with George and a nod at me, we learned all about the Kodiak king crab heyday, dating back to the 1960s and early '70s.

"King crab put Kodiak on the map," he bellowed in a deep baritone voice that carried through the tiny kitchen and out into the front yard.

"Boats from all over the world came here back then and caught millions and millions of these babies." I tried to picture millions and millions of these huge spidery creatures and wondered what purpose they had.

"What do you do with them?" asked George, always the curious.

"You eat 'em, what do you think!" answered Tom. George and I looked at each other, blinking. No way was I going to bite on that thing; I didn't care if other people wanted millions of them. "Here, I'll show ya," said Tom as he stepped over to the sink. "Get me the biggest pot you have and fill it up with water." I pulled out my stewpot and he peered at it, frowning.

"Wait a minute." Tom walked out the door, found something in his truck and walked back in, the screen door banging shut. He was carrying a stainless-steel pot the size of my mother's washtub. Wow. Everything seems so big up here, I thought. He set the pot on the stove, covering all four burners, and filled it with water using the stewpot. He turned each burner on high. Tiny bubbles rose to the surface as the water came to a boil. Tom picked up the now dead crab and carried it over to the sink.

"You'll need a garbage bag and some newspapers 'cause this is gonna get messy," said Tom. We covered the counter with newspapers as Tom tied the garbage bag to the drawer handle below the sink. "Now, here's what we do." He carefully grabbed the two back legs with one hand, fitting his fingers between the prickly spikes while he grabbed the edge of the main shell with the other hand and peeled it off the body with a crackling snap. He cracked off the front shell next and dropped it into the sink with the back shell. He gripped both sides of the crab, carefully weaving his fingers between the spikes again and broke the body in half. He demonstrated how to pull off the lungs, which are poisonous, and clean out the guts. By that time, the water was boiling hard and Tom dropped both sets of crab legs into the water.

"Twelve minutes," Tom said. "Not a minute more, not a minute less." George and I watched as the foamy water boiled around the crab legs and turned them a pale orange. "Now you'll need a roll of paper towels and melt some butter, if you like. Some people eat crab by dipping it in melted butter, but I prefer the natural taste of the crab," explained Tom. "You can try it both ways, if you like."

We liked. In fact, that was the best-tasting thing I could re-member ever eating in my life. It was delicious. It took a lot of painful practice trying to grip the legs between the spikes and snap them at each joint just right so the meat came out as a single piece. Much later, we purchased a good pair of crab scissors and cut the shells lengthwise. We used nutcrackers to open the hard-shelled claws and scraped the meat out with a fork or chopstick. Yum!

The next day, we went out with Tom in his eighteen-foot alu-minum skiff. "Let's go check the pots, Georgie, we'll see what we catch this time."

Subsistence crab pots measured four feet square, crafted by hand using rebar cut, welded together into a box-shape frame, and then covered on the sides and bottom with fishing net. A plastic ring about four inches tall was fastened to the center inside the top of the pot leaving a two-inch gap all around. A plastic jug with small holes punched in the sides was filled with bait and fastened inside the pot near the bottom. One end of a polypropylene line about one hundred feet long was tied to the top of the pot and a large round buoy was attached to the other end of the line.

We motored out in Tom's tiny metal skiff to a large orange buoy floating on the water marked with Tom's name and phone number. Tom handed George a gaff, a three-foot-long metal bar with a hook at one end.

"Grab the line dangling from that buoy as we motor close to it, and pull it to the boat." George leaned over as we drifted near it and snagged the rope, pulling the buoy next to the boat. I grabbed the buoy and lifted it over the side of the boat. "Good job, Georgie, you guys are real pros already. See that? Now let's pull the pot up and see what we got."

Suddenly halted in the water as the men held onto the waterlogged line, the small skiff was encircled by waves spilling over one side of the boat and into the bottom where it swirled hurriedly to the back of the boat and slowly drained out of the tiny hole fixed about two inches above the floor.

I stared in growing alarm as another wave hit the other side, washing up and over and spilling down and backwards again. I sat down and gripped the wooden seat with both hands, trying to steady the rocking motion, watching the water rush up and over and down and back. Then the other side, up and over and down and back.

My stomach began to join in with this lazy, rocking motion, up and over and down and back, first one side then the other, up and over and down and back. I felt the toast and eggs and bacon and orange juice from our hurried breakfast swirl around in my stomach, up and over and down and back, in time with the waves and water and swirling; up and over and down and back until I felt the whole mess rising up to my chest and into my throat. I began to sweat with chills and my hands cramped up as I gripped the rough splintery edges harder, willing the queasiness to stop. My head was pounding, my ears felt stuffed and rang with the swaying and swashing of the watery mess, up, over, down and back. I followed the unending rhythmic motion, unable to tear my eyes away from the bottom of the boat where the salty gray slosh inched up around my boots. I tried to swallow but my tongue was stuck dry to the roof of my mouth, my throat was thick and sickly warm.

"Clare!" shouted Tom, blasting through my sorry state. My head snapped up at my name to see Tom standing on the other seat looking down at me. Tom's startling yell was enough to divert my queasy thoughts and my stomach dropped back down to its normal place.

"Keep your eyes on the horizon when you're in a boat," he cautioned. "Find a land mass and focus on it every few minutes. And for Pete's sake, don't eat such a heavy breakfast next time, and you'll be okay." This useful advice I consistently adhered to from that moment on, saving me from any future bouts of seasickness.

Meanwhile, the two men stood at the bow, one in front of the other; they gripped the line and pulled up, then grabbed again. Each time, about a yard of the wet dripping line snaked to the bottom of the boat as they moved hand-over-hand, getting into a rhythm.

"Now you got it, now you got it, Georgie," said Tom swaying back and forth with his feet apart at shoulder width as he leaned over then pulled back. The boat rocked side to side as they pulled, gripped, and pulled again. On the downside, they grabbed line, on the upside they leaned back and pulled. I watched this almost comical sync with amazement while keeping one eye on the beach and rocks nearby. I found the faraway horizon, where the blue water, glittering in the sun, met the softer blue of sky, and I began to see the beauty of this place. I spotted green-headed mallards bobbing along with the waves, whitewashed seagulls soaring above and calling out their piercing song. I smiled at a brightly colored puffin with his blaze orange beak as he patted awkwardly on top of the water for several yards before lifting off to a rocky cliff nearby.

After what seemed like ages, the salty white line now coiled high like a snake basket, the heavy crab pot broke the surface of the water crowded with crabs. *Bonanza!* The pot was alive with several king crabs clipped to the insides of the net from side to side and crawling about just below the plastic ring like a nest of spiders in a corner.

Tom and Georgie heaved the pot, now weighing close to one hundred and fifty pounds, up the side of the boat and balanced it on the edge with the opening tipped downwards toward the inside of the boat. George and I, shaking with excitement, stood on each side of the pot holding it steady. Tom reached inside and carefully pulled out the crabs one by one, unhooking claws and untangling spiky sharp legs from the net and tossing them into a large plastic tote.

We motored back to shore, washed down the boat and hosed out the engine, then cleaned the crab. We enjoyed another fantastic crab feast and packed the remaining bounty into Ziploc bags, stacking them neatly in the freezer for later.

After several trips with Tom, we bought an old wooden skiff with a forty horsepower Evinrude, made three crab pots out of rebar, nets, and buoys acquired from Tom's shed, and ventured out on our own. We quickly learned that there were crab bandits out there and leaving pots unchecked for more than two days would yield nothing but a sore back.

It was the beginning of crab season the following year and after obtaining the proper subsistence licenses and making some minor repairs to the skiff, we loaded the pots, buoys, and line and motored out to our selected spot, located mostly by trial and error and a little help from Tom.

We started out catching between seven and ten crab in each pot. We were ecstatic. The water was frigid even in the summer and pulling up the heavy pots, seemingly glued to the bottom of the ocean a hundred feet below, was backbreaking work. However, the thrill of seeing all the crabs stacked inside the pot when it breached the surface was like Christmas.

Not too crabby!

Each time we went out, we got better at it. The gaff caught the buoy on the second aim, if not the first; the lines didn't get as tangled after practicing the coiling method; and we learned to watch the rim of the boat on the downward tip so the waves didn't wash over the side so much. We gradually developed "sea legs" and gained a sense of boat balance, and each trip became an exciting adventure until the bandits appeared.

It was late June when the pots started coming up empty. We carefully baited and dropped each pot in the same location using the landmarks Tom told us about, but the crabs were just not in the pots. At that time, GPS was not available, so anglers used charts, mountaintops, bays, rock outcroppings, and offshore rocks for points of reference to estimate locations on the water.

We diligently hooked onto the buoys, grabbed the line and with the rhythmic motion of rocking the boat side to side, hauled up each pot about twice a week. Nothing. The crab pot bandits had beaten us to them.

Some bandits were actually courteous. They would at least rebait the pots, and one time a bandit left a six-pack of Coors in the bottom of the pot. We never caught the pot bandits but we learned to relocate the pots occasionally and check them more often. After that, we usually caught enough crab for ourselves and acquired a new fitness program in the deal.

Tom and his lovely wife eventually moved back to their hometown in Maine, for better jobs, they said. We learned from a letter received a few years later from Tom's wife that Tom never really adjusted to the big city life. Tom found it difficult to navigate the maze of roads, maneuver the one-and-a-half-hour commute to and from work, and tolerate the constant crime in the news along with the general dinginess and blaring noise of the place. One day, Tom was killed in a car accident. They had just been planning a visit back to Kodiak, she had written, but it would not happen now.

As we ate the last crab of that season, we made a toast to Tom, the Crab King.

3 JUST PLAIN LUCKY

Complacency was not easily forgiven in a place where a single day's adventure could take one even farther into a vast wilderness. A seemingly minor mistake was often fatal.

It was late September two years later. The once brilliant green leaves were fading, the tiny edges curling upwards, wrinkled and crispy brown. The hardy, thick blankets of wild grasses and weeds were limp with heavy dew, and the fireweed blossoms blazed red-orange, announcing the end of summer and the beginning of the crisp, cool fall season.

We were all feeling lucky as we started out on a routine day of fishing on the ocean just off the coast on the west side of the island with a friend of ours named Matt.

Matt was five feet six inches and weighed about one hundred eighty pounds, with dark curly hair drooping past his collar, brown button eyes set too close together on a long weathered face with a constant grin. He wore a brown grubby fishing vest over a tattered flannel shirt and faded blue jeans tucked into brown rubber knee boots. He also wore a consistently happy-go-lucky attitude that kept you upbeat for a while, and then became annoying when things needed to be serious. He lived in a cottage down the street from ours and quickly became a frequent visitor at our place. George had repaired some electrical outlets and switches in Matt's house a few weeks before, so Matt invited us to go fishing on his eighteen-foot orange and white Glassply cabin cruiser.

Matt was full of great stories of his boyhood growing up in Kodiak. He told fascinating tales of catching big, flat, floppy fish the size of a sheet of plywood, camping out on distant island beaches, and numerous showdowns with huge Kodiak brown bears. All the cool stuff he had done on the island was fascinating.

The day was clear, calm, and sunny with a slight breeze coming from the south, perfect for a day on the ocean. We had a few fish in the box by late afternoon and decided to head for a nearby island. It was a small, out-of-the-way place with a quiet cove and a nice sandy beachhead. We often went ashore there to relax and explore the beaches for any treasures we could find.

Matt cut the engine and the boat eased onto the sandy beach as George climbed to the front of the boat and positioned the anchor on the edge of the bow. We leaped off into the shallow water, Matt holding the other end of the anchor line while George and I shoved hard on the boat, pushing it back off the beach into water deep enough to make it out past the surf dragging the attached line through the water.

Matt watched the boat slide back to the ocean for a few moments then yanked hard on the line. The anchor jerked off the bow and splashed into the water, caught on the bottom, and the boat slowed to a stop. Waves lapped gently against the sides as the boat floated taut on the line. We turned and waded back to the beach, George and I with our backpacks firmly fixed to our shoulders, Matt with nothing.

"I don't know why you guys brought all that stuff ashore, we're only going to be here for a while," Matt said as he walked up the beach dragging the boat line.

"Ya never know, Matt, we might get hungry or somethin'," answered George.

"Nah, why bother," Matt flipped a hand in the air and kicked at a scallop shell half buried in the sand. We looked at each other, shrugged our shoulders and kept on walking. We had at least learned one thing in this land of so-called opportunity: if you didn't bring it, you ain't got it.

Matt dragged the line over to a dead tree, tied it to a branch and began walking up the shore.

"Hey Matt, do you think that branch is gonna hold? It looks a bit weak for the boat line," George said. Matt didn't bother to turn around.

"Nah, it's good enough. That boat ain't going nowhere. Let's go on up to that ridge and see if we can spot some deer."

"Sure," George said.

We hefted our packs and began climbing up through the alders, tall grasses, and spruce trees, making our way past mossy hills and smelling the fresh salty air that always made me smile. Ah, this was nature at its best! Not to be duplicated in any room spray, candle, or potpourri, that's for sure. I inhaled a deep long breath and let it out slowly.

We continued to climb for about half an hour. Close to the top, we stepped out onto a grassy ledge and gazed at the breathtaking scenery. The entire view was a picture-perfect painting of sparkling blue water, clear blue sky and varied shades of green mountains that seem sculpted like Japanese topiary trees. The closest one appeared to be in the shape of a large whale, aptly named Whale Island.

There were fourteen main islands and a few small stubs that make up the Kodiak Archipelago, formed millions of years ago by volcanoes and glacial erosions. Gradually, vegetation took over; animals arrived by crossing the ancient land bridge from other continents or brought ashore by ancient settlers or Russian hunters and missionaries who began arriving in the late 1700s. Trees were nonexistent on southern parts of the islands. The

north side of Kodiak and Afognak Island were covered with
Sitka spruce, cottonwoods and dense thickets of willow, alder,
and elderberry.

We stood at the edge of the cliff gazing at the sheer beauty
of the uninhabited wilderness and vast expanse of blue ocean,
drinking in a sight made for memories—one of those that you
gaze at for a long time, taking in as much as you can, so you
never forget the beauty of the moment. I soaked in the vibrant
colors, the tangy smells and the wonders of nature and heartily
agreed with John Muir and the early naturalists, who proclaimed
that nature filled one's spirit and cleansed the soul.

The three of us silently scanned the azure horizon of ocean-
meets-sky, enjoying the beauty, when George's neck suddenly
jerked forward and one hand shot to his forehead to shade the
sun. He peered intensely at a dot of orange and white—a boat
drifting out towards the channel. A boat that looked a lot like the
one we'd just come out of.

George whipped around to Matt. "Hey, isn't that your boat
drifting out there? Out there, to the left of that outcropping."
He pointed his arm straight out at the small colorful dot moving
farther away inch by inch.

"Nah, it can't be my boat, it's anchored over there somewhere," said Matt with a careless flick of his hand. We followed
the flick to the east where the sandy beach lay and the boat used
to be. We turned our heads at the same time back towards the
boat, which we could just barely see as it drifted farther and
farther out to sea. Judging by the direction it was heading, figuring in the tides and wind current, the boat should reach Russia
in about two days.

"George! We gotta get down there now!" yelled Matt.
"That's my boat headed out there! Run, George!" The three of
us scrambled back down the hillside, dodging trees, leaping logs
and stumps, and running as fast as we could down, down, down
to the shore. The faster we ran, the more we stumbled, fell, and
got back up and ran again. Branches, bushes, and thorns tore at

our clothes and painfully scratched bare skin, until finally we reached the shore.

Standing together, with our hands up to our brows and heaving great gulps of air back into our lungs, we watched anxiously as the boat, dragging the line and with the branch still attached, rode the outgoing tide, slowly but surely, in the direction of Russia.

"Go, George, go! Get out there now! Swim out to the boat, quick, before it gets out of the channel!" Matt flapped his arms up and down and stomped back and forth in anxious fits. We both turned to Matt, blinked our eyes a couple of times, trying to decide if he was serious. Apparently, he was. He kept shouting and pointing and finally pushed George on the shoulder. "Go get the boat, go get the boat, George!"

Now, despite being an expert swimmer back in high school, neither George nor anybody in his right mind would swim out there to catch that boat. The boat was now at least two hundred yards from the beach. And this was Kodiak. By the time a person swam half that distance without protective suit and gear, he would be hypothermic from the frigid thirty-four-degree water and then die, sink to the bottom, and become crab food.

"No way, Matt, I'm not doing that. You go for it, if you think you can make it. I'll watch from here," said George.

"Me? Are you crazy? I can't even swim, let alone get that far!" Matt stammered and stomped his feet while George and I exchanged a look of raised eyebrows.

The fact that he couldn't swim was a big surprise. He claimed to be the big fishing king of Kodiak, said he wrestled bears with his bare hands, caught more fish than anyone on earth, and swum with the whales since he was a kid. So he claimed. *Jeez. Great. Just spiffy. Lesson number 985: when people brag so much that they can do stuff, you can pretty well figure that they can't do it at all.*

George and I turned around and started back up towards the edge of the woods. We stopped at a large pale log, worn clean and smooth from years of weathering saltwater tides and harsh winter storms. We sat down, opened our backpacks and took out sandwiches and water. Matt finally noticed we weren't still standing next him and trudged back up the sandy beach and stopped in front of us.

"What are you doing?" he asked.

George looked up as he chewed, swallowed, then answered. "Eatin' lunch."

Several seconds passed before Matt brought himself to ask. "Got anything for me?"

"Where's your pack, Matt?"

"On the boat. I guess I forgot it." Matt sighed.

"Bummer."

We continued chewing our thick slices of whole wheat bread stuffed with ham and pepper jack cheese, my favorite. Matt's head twitched from George to me and back to George trying to figure out which of us would be the generous one, who would be the easiest to talk out of a sandwich. We leisurely finished eating and stuffed the wrappers back in the packs.

Matt's hangdog face was getting pathetic but George stalled a bit longer, enjoying the moment. He fiddled with his boot cuffs, then smoothed out his shirtsleeves, then repositioned his ball cap. Finally, he fumbled around inside his pack and pulled out another sandwich.

"Here." George held out the sandwich to Matt. "You won't be any good to us if you starve to death out here. Eat it and let's get going."

Matt grabbed the sandwich, tore off the plastic wrap, and took two large bites. "Going where?" Matt garbled from one side of his mouth, most of the sandwich still in his cheek.

"Well, I don't know about you, Matt, but I'm planning on making camp." George stood up and hoisted the pack onto his shoulders.

"Making camp? Why are you doing that? The boat will come back; all we have to do is wait for the next tide."

"OK, you wait for the next tide, we're gonna make camp. It's getting cold and the sun will be gone in about two hours." It was Matt's turn to blink his eyes, caught between his usual cockiness about everything being just peachy, and wondering if it really was.

George quickly scanned the area, and then moved toward a clump of trees. The roots of a huge fallen tree stuck out over the sand. "This'll do. Gather some of those big branches over there and start stacking them up next to this stump."

I reached around to the pack stuck to my back, pulled out a pair of gloves from the side pouch, and slipped them on. I walked into the woods, grabbed two long spruce branches off the ground—conveniently discarded by the friendly giant trees—and dragged them over to the stump.

George brought over more branches and together we began stacking them up around the dead tree roots. Weaving the more pliable branches, we tucked them around and over the top of the roots, making a basket-like shelter. Then we placed more branches over the sand inside the shelter. Next, we gathered deadwood and stacked it next to the stump until we had enough to start a fire.

George reached in his backpack and pulled out a small yellow waterproof container. He unsnapped the lid and took out one match and one small roll of twine. He carefully laid the twine next to a few dried leaves and tiny twigs and pine needles. He scratched the tip of the match with his thumbnail and moved it around the small gathering of kindling. With the expertise of a seasoned camper, he gently placed larger sticks, a few at a time, in teepee fashion around the tiny blaze. When those caught, he strategically placed more sticks and then a couple of small branches.

The fire was going strong when Matt showed up. Already knowing the answer, George asked anyway.

"Did your boat show up?"

Matt shook his head with a frown. "No, not yet, but it'll show up anytime now." His frown quickly changed to his goofy, optimistic grin that by now had become annoying.

I was only mildly concerned at the time, since we had enough food and survival items to last a couple of days. But who knew how long we would be out here. Still, if all else failed, someone would call the Coast Guard. We'd left word with our friend Jim about where we were going, always a wise thing to do when traveling anywhere, but even more so around Kodiak. There were so many hazards that could happen, it was best to be prepared.

I began to wonder if Matt had already forgotten everything he'd learned about Kodiak, or if he'd ever known anything in the first place. Maybe he just didn't care. Probably the latter, since somehow things always worked out for him. Personally, I couldn't leave that much to luck, but he'd managed to get by on it for years. Some people are like that.

It was close to midnight by now and darkness was coming on fast as we began setting up sleeping supplies. Matt watched with apparent curiosity and then sauntered over with his happy grin.

"Say, you guys, this little hooch looks real cozy. What side do I get?"

We glanced at each other, thinking the same thing. Should we let him in? He didn't help build it, he didn't come prepared and now he wanted to share our stuff. Jeez. George slowly turned to Matt.

"Gee, Matt, I don't know. There's really only enough room for us. You might want to try that tree stump a bit farther down the beach," said George, gesturing vaguely to the left of our camp.

"Ah, come on, there's plenty of room for all of us, I won't take up much room. Look, see? I'll just lie over on this side." He walked over the sleeping bags and pulled one over to a corner, leaving a gap. His head bumped the branches above and pine needles rained down all over the bedding.

"Oops. Guess someone is gonna get a bit prickly tonight," he grinned sheepishly. In five seconds, he managed to track sand over the blankets, knock pine needles on the sleeping bags and step right on the backpacks, totally destroying the neat little sleeping shelter that had taken us a half an hour to build.

I quickly looked over at George and could see the telltale signs: the clenched jaw, the narrowed eyes and the fisted hands flexing ever so slightly. I swiftly stepped over to my sleeping bag, pulled out the blanket wrapped inside and tossed it at Matt.

"Here, Matt, you can use this blanket and wrap up in the tarp and make your own sleeping bag. It'll keep out the moisture and the blanket is wool, so you should be nice and warm." Matt glanced at George, noted the scowl and readily agreed.

"Sure this'll be great. This'll be just fine for me."

I pulled George's sleeping bag back in place, shifted everything over about two feet, leaving room for Matt to layer the blanket and tarp into a bedroll.

"It'll be warmer if everyone stays close together for the night," I said as I smoothed out the bedding and resettled our stuff along the edges of the blanket.

I stole a sideways glance at George as I brushed away the pine needles and sand. I gave him a brief smile with raised eyebrows, urging him to move on and make the best of it. He slowly relaxed, pulled his face in a crooked smile and rolled his eyes. I knew exactly what he was thinking, but I didn't want him to say it, at least not now. We had other problems to worry about.

Lying awake, watching the stars flicker in between the branches of our shelter, I couldn't help wondering how someone who always said how much he knew about everything around here could, in this time of crisis, be so unprepared. Perhaps my interpretation of a seasoned fisherman in Kodiak was a tad different. Perhaps it just meant you could catch a lot of fish, and that was it.

To me, you had to get there in a boat, so you should know about boats. You needed to be prepared for rough water, so you should have working emergency equipment on board. You never knew what was going to happen once you got out there, so basic survival skills should be ingrained in your head. And everything you might need, in case something goes wrong, should be on your back. I closed my eyes tight, trying to shut out these irritating thoughts about this self-proclaimed expert. I inhaled and exhaled slowly, twice.

My mind shifted to thoughts of our past life of brightly lit shopping malls, stores filled with colorful racks of new clothes, long aisles of sophisticated shoes marching along shelves, manicured lawns and sparkling sidewalks, paved streets teeming with shiny cars and chattering people and . . . choking smog and head-pounding frantic racket.

I jerked my thoughts back to the present, back to the inky black sky dotted with silvery stars, the peaceful silence of the night, and back to the immediate problem of holding onto an "upbeat and positive" attitude despite the gnawing notion that we were stranded. At least George was prepared. We had lived in Kodiak for only a few years, but he had learned a lot. And taught me, as well.

I wondered at this strange new world I had come to. Mother Nature ruled—big, bold, and present in all her wondrous beauty— but she was nasty and vicious at times, unmerciful to those who didn't listen and learn and prepare for her constant change of heart.

This was the essence of Kodiak. With fewer than seven thousand people year round, there were no traffic jams, no crowds, and no major crime. Of course, there were no malls, no major highways, and no predictable weather for more than a few hours at a time, either. It was a place where inconveniences were taken in stride, modern technology lay in the distant future, and surviving the elements became the focus for the island's stalwart inhabitants.

I thought of the positives: A person could fish, hunt, hike, or just sit and watch glossy black ravens and bald eagles soaring overhead or perching in trees calling to each other. Sea lions, seals, otters, whales, and puffins could be seen from the boat on most fishing trips. And the fishing was excellent with five species of salmon as well as cod, sea bass, herring and the king of fish, halibut. All these facts and images of nature flipped through my mind like a tourist brochure as I drifted off to sleep. Tomorrow would be another day.

And it came with a fury! The winds howled, the rain poured down and the wild surf pounded onto the beach, clawing back sand and water in great curls of dirty, angry foam. George and I woke at the same time when branches of spruce, whisked away by the wind, left a gap in our "roof" and rain suddenly spat in our faces.

I clambered to my feet, swiped water-drenched hair from my face and stared in total astonishment as George jumped over to the still sleeping Matt, with one quick motion grabbed two fist-fuls of tarp, and jerked hard and up. The tarp came free as Matt rolled out like a spinning hot dog, out through the opening and down the rain-soaked beach.

"Grab an end and weave the tarp through the top branches, quick!" shouted George. I hurriedly started tucking in the edges of the tarp up and around the insides of the branches to form a lining above our heads as I listened to shouts from Matt.

He came fully awake, jumped up shaking his hands, flapping his arms, stamping his feet, and twirling around shouting curses and acting like a crazy man. He was totally shocked and decid-edly useless to us now. I kept my eyes averted, moving my hands quickly and busily tucking sections of tarp along the gaps.

Repairs completed, George pulled his rain gear out and slipped it on. I worked myself into my rain jacket and pants, and stood next to him watching the rain dance. Matt suddenly stopped, turned, and ran back inside the shelter, still cussing and sputtering, his long johns drenched and stuck to his skin, his hair pasted flat to his dripping head.

"How could you do that?" yelled Matt. "What were you thinking?" He stomped one foot, then the other, his hands balled into fists. Nobody answered. George's face was expressionless except for a small twitch in the corner of his mouth as we looked at the drowned rat in front of us. I had no such compassion. I let back and roared with laughter. It was too funny.

As bouncing back from any crisis was one of Matt's strong points, he began to laugh too. The three of us laughed long and hard while the rain beat down on the ground outside our meager but slightly drier shelter. Tension released, we chuckled back to normal as George took out a pair of extra clothes from his pack and tossed them to Matt.

Then the laughter halted as we came back to our present gloomy situation. Out towards the beach, the storm raged violently on, moving slowly to the east. To the west, the skies were clearing slightly; a thin line of pale white lay across the horizon gently nudging away the heavy dark clouds. It appeared the storm would pass over soon; we just had to wait it out. Lucky us. Our shared supplies were dwindling.

In good spirits, we sat down in the middle of the makeshift enclosure and searched our backpacks for breakfast. I had one sandwich, two bagels slathered with peanut butter, four trail mix bars and three bottles of water. George sorted out two baggies of smoked fish, two packs of crackers, one pack of beef jerky and four bottles of water.

Matt looked on, his shoulders slumped, head down, humbled and on his best behavior. He hoped for a handout and quickly forgave his purported ill treatment.

"Gee, George, you really came prepared. I can see that. It's best to be prepared when you come out here, I always say. That's the smart thing to do. You never know what might happen. You should always hope for the best and plan for the worst. That's what a real Alaskan does, that's good survival advice, you know.

I can see you picked up on that real quick since you've been here." George looked hard at Matt, hoping his words would bounce off his forehead and back into Matt's own head. There was always hope.

The rain subsided and white clouds appeared, allowing sun to shine down in scattered patches of yellow-white beams like spotlights from heaven. We stepped outside the branch tent and peered up at the sky. I followed a spotlight downward to the horizon. There to the left, just a speck of white shone on the water. It grew larger and larger.

"Hey, what's that on the water?" I pointed. "Way out there about ten o'clock, past that rock pile." The three of us took a few steps towards the shore and stared, shielding our eyes with both hands. George darted back into the shelter and returned with binoculars.

He peered through the lenses and after several minutes, silently passed them to me with a small smile. I stuck them to my face, finding the mysterious object through the magnified eyes, then smiled as well, passing the binoculars over to Matt.

"Looks like the Lone Ranger is coming to the rescue," I said. "What do you think, Matt?"

He took the field glasses from me and peered at the boat, getting larger and more distinct. "Dang!" he shouted, still wearing the binoculars. "I think its Jerry. Yep, it's Jerry all right. Anybody but Jerry! I'll never hear the end of it now. What's he doing here? I wish it were anybody else." He threw the binoculars to the ground. "This is the pits! Dang and double dang times two!" he ranted, his arms jerking wildly about, his feet kicking clouds of sand in the air as he stomped around in a circle.

"Yo, Matt. He's coming to save us. Get some grateful in ya and let's pack up," said George as he picked up the binoculars and wiped off the sand. "I'm not willing to stay on this beach any longer; I don't care who it is."

"Hey to the shore, hey to the shore! You guys missing anything? Like a boat, maybe?" We could hear Jerry laughing from the open window on his boat. Matt's boat was towing happily behind Jerry's, looking none the worse for wear, and a mighty good sight for wet, cold, and hungry eyes. George and I waved eagerly back at Jerry.

"Hi Jerry, nice to see you. Nice to see you, for sure!" I waved rapidly back and forth with both arms, happy and relieved. Matt's shoulders slumped with embarrassment but unmistakable relief appeared on his face.

"Saw this boat drifting past my camp, just bobbing in the water, nobody in it, and thought about you guys. Decided you could probably use a lift. Not that this boat wouldn't have eventually made it back to you in, oh, give or take the tides and all, probably about a month. Next time, you might want to tie it to a bigger branch," Jerry said, looking hard at Matt.

Jerry camped in a small cabin during fishing season, just over on the next island. He was a rough, salty dog kind of guy, burly, bald, and about the most sea-smart person we had ever met. Not too friendly, but he seemed to appear when you needed him. Uncanny, that. We'd encountered his kindness before, but he never explained and never accepted anything but a "thank you."

One of the lifelong residents of this remote Alaskan island, Jerry knew the waters around Kodiak better than most. He knew about all the hidden underwater rocks that other boats invariably plowed into during low tide and he could navigate in the foggiest weather and instinctively knew when the weather would change, just in time to make for shore. Few other people we knew could read clouds, air pressure, and wind direction like Jerry. All this made for quick and drastic changes in ocean waves, bringing soupy blankets of fog and the dreaded over-the-bow whitecaps that came up out of nowhere, making many a seaworthy boat tip and dive like a duck in a whirlpool bath.

We waded out, climbed aboard and offered profusions of thanks, reimbursements for fuel, and invitations for dinner at our house at his earliest convenience, and everything else we thought he might like. He smiled briefly, accepted nothing, looked over each of us, then his eyes locked on George.

"You all okay?"

George smiled back. "Just fine." They held eyes for a moment longer, each reading the other completely. Nodding once, Jerry turned and started the engine.

We sat quietly on the way home, each in our own thoughts. I was grateful for the rescue, although I rather enjoyed the adventure, the uppermost thought being, however, that there would not have been any enjoyment at all if we had not been prepared. I looked sideways at Matt. His face was sullen, one could say almost thoughtful. I was hoping he had learned a few lessons himself, but I wasn't totally convinced. It seemed he was just too lucky to learn.

Some said it was better to be lucky than smart. I hoped to be a little of both. One without the other would leave little control over survival or no real enjoyment in those quirky, unpredictable events that made up life.

4 CLOSE NEIGHBORS

I was wrong. We came home from work one day and found a glaring pink sheet of paper tacked to the door telling us to move. It stated that our cottage would be demolished along with several others to make way for a new housing development. We packed up our belongings once again in brown cardboard boxes and loaded them in the truck. At least it would be a local move. George was not ready to leave Kodiak—not yet.

It was a drizzling soggy day in July when we purchased a 14-by-70-foot mobile home located in a small park that consisted of sixteen look-alikes, making up two rows sitting side by side and front to back. How fortunate that we now lived only a few yards from Jerry!

For a monthly fee, the tiny park offered running water, sewer, phone hookups, and zero privacy, but at least we owned the trailer. We met a hardy cast of characters, who mostly kept to themselves unless they needed something, or wanted to know what you were doing, or where you came from, or why you drove a Chevy instead of a Ford.

One such character was Old Carl. Each winter starting about the middle of December through the end of February, we woke suddenly at midnight and then at two-hour intervals as the old man next door started up his old van, parked by our bedroom window, to keep it from freezing in the subzero temperatures. George offered to install a block heater, like other people used, but the crusty old-timer kept it his way. Inevitably, the park dogs would sit up and sing their own chorus of howls, barks, and yaps for the first fifteen minutes. Blackie learned to chime in as well, and then all was silent until the van roared to life again two hours later. We learned to stuff our ears with cotton and earplugs, like other people. I wore a snowcap to bed as well and soon got used to it.

The man two trailers down had a cat that would appear on our doorstep every evening just after dinner, like some sort of ritual. Blackie and George ignored him; I obediently set out a saucer of milk with pieces of bread crusts. The cat would sit there patiently for sometimes an hour waiting for his due. When he had cleaned the saucer, his face, and his two front paws, he sauntered back to his own trailer.

Kodiak was a small, friendly town in those days. Few people bothered to lock their doors and the car keys were always in the cars. We relaxed to the same complacency, since few crimes ever appeared in the newspaper.

I was mildly confused then, when I woke on a Sunday morning and padded out to the kitchen. I grabbed a mug from the hooks on the wall and reached for the coffeepot. It wasn't there. Still stupid from sleep, I looked around the kitchen, even opened a few cabinet doors. Nothing. No coffeepot. I could smell fresh coffee, just couldn't find the pot. I was puzzled, baffled and finally annoyed enough to awaken George.

I stomped back to the bedroom and shook the long lump of blanket.

"George, George. Wake up." I nudged him.

"Hmm." mumbled George. He rolled over inside the fleecy mound and started to snore.

"George. Wake up!" I persisted.

"What?" groaned George with his eyes still shut.

"George, there is no coffee."

"Well, can't you just make some?" He slowly turned his head to me, eyes blinking awake.

"I can't make coffee, George. There's no coffeepot." I tried to keep my voice an even monotone, but my impatience seeped out around the edges.

It took only a few seconds for it to sink in. George's eyes flew open; he flicked back the blankets, sat up and pulled on some clothes from the floor. I jumped out of his way as he stomped down the narrow hallway and out the door.

I frowned as he headed around the back of the trailer, punched through the row of bushes separating the trailers behind us, and stomped up the stairs of Jerry's trailer and across the deck to the door. He pounded hard enough to wake up the other fifteen trailer residents.

"Jerry. Jerry! Open up," shouted George. New to the trailer park, we still abided by the courtesy of knocking and waiting for the occupant to open the door, or at least give permission to enter. However, after two beats, George opened the door himself and walked inside.

"Where's the coffeepot, Jerry?" asked George.

"Oh, it's right over there. Wanna cup?" Jerry spoke in calm, quiet tones, gesturing to the counter where his coffeemaker held our coffeepot.

"No. I want my coffeepot back!"

"Well, aren't we cranky in the morning? And here I was being so quiet and not waking you two up," Jerry reasoned.

He was a solid, chunky man, five feet eight inches with small brown eyes stuck in a round pudgy face with a permanent scowl on his broad forehead. He was mostly bald with peppered brown fringe running around the middle part of his head and a few strands combed desperately over the top. He lived alone except for a scraggly orange and white cat named Meathead (of all things). The cat was just as cantankerous as Jerry, and wore the same scowl on its rangy face—a real Garfield look-alike.

Jerry also had an annoying habit of "borrowing" stuff and not bringing it back. George knew right where the coffeepot had gone. Other times George had spotted a tool or rake or lawn chair around Jerry's yard and had to carry it back to our place. But the coffeepot theft was the last straw.

George took a quick deep breath, preparing to let loose a fury. He grabbed the pot and turned to Jerry wielding it like a weapon. Jerry had pasted a small humble smile on his face that was so unusual George stopped in his tracks in stunned confusion.

"I slipped this morning when I was carrying my pot to the sink for water and it broke in a million pieces," Jerry explained in a never-before-heard pitiful voice. It was then that George noticed the large white bandage wrapped clumsily around Jerry's right hand. His eyes took in the broom in the corner with the dustpan filled with pieces of glass and a chunk of the black plastic handle. "And I was up at five a.m. this morning and I know how you two like to sleep in on Sundays and I was careful to be real quiet and you see I didn't wake anyone up, although Blackie gave me one of his weird looks," Jerry continued in this unusually quiet monologue.

George slowly let the air out of his mouth and happened to look down at the cat. It was sitting neatly next to Jerry, tail curled around its paws in a perfect pose wearing the same pitiful expression. The cat slowly lifted a front paw and delicately licked the pads and slicked down the orange fur over his toes, as if emphasizing this sorry state of affairs.

George blinked back the strange twilight thoughts, breathed out the last of his fury through his nose, and headed for the door.

"Come on over in a few minutes, Jerry. We'll make a fresh pot," said George. He brought the coffeepot back in the house, scooped in the fixings and turned the switch on. We looked at each other; George rolled his eyes and shook his head. Relieved my coffee cup would soon be filled, I headed for the shower.

Getting dressed in the bedroom, I heard the front door push open and the familiar obnoxious bellow.

"Hey, that coffee smells good. What's for breakfast? Isn't Mudiver up yet, it's almost noon. She sleepin' the day away again?" Jerry jerked a chair out from the kitchen table and plopped down, laying his injured hand in plain sight for anticipated sympathy.

"She's been up already, Jerry, looking for the coffeepot," answered George, his eyes locking on Jerry's face in unspoken warning. Jerry looked down at his hand, gingerly fixing and tucking the bandage with his other hand, setting up a painful expression on his face as he heard me come into the kitchen.

"Good morning, Jerry," I said in my cheeriest greeting. I was getting used to his ways and often used the 'kill him with kindness' tactic that seemed to tame down his persistent snarl. "Nice of you to drop by. Have you eaten yet? I'm just starting breakfast for George, how do you like your eggs?" Not waiting for the answer I already knew, I began pulling out the fixings - eggs, bacon, plates, and pan. George plugged in the toaster, popped in two slices of bread, and put the butter on the table. Apparently preferring food rather than sympathy, Jerry gave up the pained look and replaced it with a pleasant grin.

"Yeh, yeh, I guess I could go for something to eat. Make mine over-easy with just barely runny yolks and I could go for some of that strawberry jam with my toast. Yeh, that sounds good. Maybe I'm a little hungry after all."

It was that way with Jerry. One minute he was as mean and grouchy as a territorial bear, the next he was just as pleasant as pie. The problem was one never knew which side of him would show up at any given moment. George saw the intelligence and energy behind the gruff, prickly exterior; I saw a challenge to smooth Jerry out occasionally, disconcerting him with kindness.

5 WAITING

In Kodiak there seemed to be a lot of waiting. Not like the waiting in other places, not like waiting for a bus or waiting in traffic or waiting in line at a retail store.

Everyone waited for the tide to come in or the tide to go out; waited for the first salmon to arrive in May; waited for the frigid, dark winters to melt into cool, daylight springs and even longer daylight summers. We waited several days for dense fog to lift off the trees and hillsides and ocean waters; we waited weeks for the rain to stop (an unofficial record one year of 41 days); we waited three hours in a tree one time for a bear to finish his long lunch of fresh salmon at the river just below us; waited months for the winter accumulation of snow to melt down to the ground again in April. We waited hours and sometimes days for the winds to die down and waves to smooth out enough to launch boats on to the ocean or the fog to lift to the required 500 feet visibility so airplanes could land and take off again. We waited months for catalog orders to arrive by barge from the "lower 48," delivering much needed parts and supplies to repair machines, vehicles, boat engines and generators (the wait could be cut to just weeks if one was desperate enough to pay the exorbitant cost of air freight). Sometimes we waited days for a technician to fly over from the mainland to repair a complex piece of equipment, usually having to do with electronics. For this reason, Kodiak people tended to stick with basic equipment, stuff that could be taken apart and put back together by a handyman (which most everyone became, sooner or later). The saying "you own it, you fix it" was born in Kodiak; it couldn't be more applicable. We waited for the inevitable disasters. The community practiced diligently each year on how to survive earthquakes, tsunamis and oil spills, fine-tuning the lessons learned from past incidents. One could set a watch by the test-warning siren that blared every Wednesday at two o'clock.

George and I waited for the fish to hit the net on an overcast day. The sky of pearl gray blended seamlessly with the gray water, almost obscuring the horizon. I had no idea what waited ahead.

6 STELLAR PERFORMANCE

It was the end of May 1988. The red salmon were making their way from their four-year ocean wanderings back towards the rivers, and we were sitting on a gillnet laid out in the bay near the mouth of the Buskin River.

The net stretched out one hundred fifty feet by twelve feet deep. A half-inch line woven through the length of one edge of the net connected small oval white cork floats the size of softballs at three-foot intervals. Another line, made of woven cotton covering a semi flexible lead rod, ran through the bottom edge of the net to weigh it down, creating a "fence" when stretched out on the water. A beach ball-sized buoy was attached at each end of the float line, with a small anchor on one end and a six-foot pull line extending from the other, kept the boat attached to the net.

George slowed the skiff about a hundred yards from shore, where I dropped the anchor and first buoy off the bow. The net slid across the bow and dropped into the water as George steered slowly out from the first buoy in a straight line. On the first two sets, the net became a tangled mass as it pulled off the boat and dragged itself into the water, causing hours of precious time lost to fixing the snags. It wasn't until we watched another boat and noted how two fishermen hauled in their net and neatly stacked it, floats on the left and lead line on the right that we finally figured it out.

With the last of the net pulled off the bow, this time without tangles, George cut the engine and glided back around as I tossed the second buoy into the water and tied the pull line to the bow cleat. It would be another half hour before the tide drifted back toward shore so I poured two cups of coffee from the thermos and glanced at the line of floats calmly bobbing in the gentle heave and ho of the ocean.

It was slack tide inside the bay with a mild current, the waves gently rising at easy intervals, making the floats appear like a dotted centerline of a highway. Overhead a Coast Guard C-130 aircraft buzzed towards the nearby runway, dropping down so close we ducked our heads, laughing and waving to the pilots.

U. S. Coast Guard C-130 rolling to the hangar

A sudden surge on the middle section of floats made us stop in midsip and midsentence. They'd hit! The net dipped down below the surface, four or five floats disappeared completely, and the water churned with fins and tails.

"We got somethin'! Quick, untie and let's go," George shouted as he yanked the pull string on the engine. The motor roared to life as I ripped off the pull line from the cleat and pushed off the buoy, nosing the bow away from the net. George whooshed down the line of floats, and then eased up to the section of net wobbling vigorously with our first catch of the day.

I grabbed a handful of net and held on while George cut the engine and swung the handle sideways, steering the back end away from the net and pulling up the prop. I leaned over the bow, bent at the waist with my hips pressed into the top edge of the metal rail, and reached down into the icy cold water for the floats now completely submerged and jerking with the weight of salmon tugging and spinning in the net. I carefully clawed up the net one handful at a time so as not to tear the mesh or lose any fish. As it reached the surface, the fish leaped, flopped, and thrashed around in one last valiant effort, sending a shower of water on me that drenched my entire upper body with a shocking chill. I counted six, maybe seven silvery swirls. As each one reached the bow, I carefully pulled the tangled mess up and over the edge, quickly untangled the gills and tails, and flipped the hard-won fish into the bucket. I dropped the net carefully back into the water, adjusting the floats back into their straight dotted line.

It was important to work swiftly before the fish could untangle themselves and swim away. Each fish meant a meal on the table for the long winter months ahead. It meant a cure for the cravings of smoked salmon—or grilled salmon, salmon salad sandwiches made from canned salmon, and our favorite, deviled eggs stuffed with salmon—in the dead of winter when the fish were no more, the rivers frozen, and the last bear had gone to bed.

It meant tasting the sweet fruits of hard work in making and maintaining the nets, sitting in a skiff in cold wind in rain-soaked clothes and tolerating the feel of frigid water up to your shoulders along with sliced fingers and bruised knuckles from the floats smashing your hands against the metal sides of the boat. It meant the inevitable bone-sore muscles you felt the next day from heaving the waterlogged net and stuffing it back into a four-foot tote that weighed one hundred and fifty pounds.

"It's all good," George would say, after all the fish were cleaned, wrapped, and packed into the freezer. We had fifteen salmon in the bucket so far, so it was indeed good.

It was nearing the end of the day and close to the regulation time for pulling in the net when I noticed one float missing from the dotted line at the far end.

"Let's continue down the line and see if we have any more stragglers before we pull up," said George. I wasn't sure if we had anything or the constant staring at the sparkling water was playing tricks on my eyes, but I wanted one more look as well.

I untied the pull line, grabbed the top of a float and pulled it behind me, grabbed another and pulled and that way we slowly moved along the net, peering down through the clear water looking for any silver streaks. We were close to the end when I spotted the shining shape caught near the very bottom that had caused the float to drop out of line. I signaled to George with my hand so he could turn the motor to the side and steer the prop away from the net while I hung on to the float until the boat was at a forty-five-degree angle.

With practiced routine, I stood up at the bow, leaned over at the waist, braced my hips on the edge and leaned down into the water. I plunged my arms in up to my shoulders and felt only minor shock as my skin quickly numbed at the icy attack. I began pulling up the net nice and easy while thoughts of the soon to be tasty smoked meat of my favorite species made my mouth water.

Closer and closer the fish rose towards the surface as I grasped handfuls of net, gently pulling up, first one hand then the other. I could see the fish clearly now, wiggling and twisting back and forth, its gills entangled in a nest of green string, twirling in one direction, then the other with acrobatic maneuvers as it struggled to get free. It was a battle of wills as we fought each other, his frightened bug-eyes staring desperately at me as he struggled to be free while I looked back with sparkling, predatory eyes. He was mine, all mine.

I concentrated on each movement of my hands, selecting just enough net, pulling up a little at a time, keeping my eyes glued to my prize as he came closer and closer until he reached the surface at last. I grabbed the fat fish firmly with one hand, my arm jerking back and forth, as I struggled to hang on to the slippery thing and tried to untangle it with my other hand at the same time. The fish flailed, flapped, and flung itself in all directions while I clamped on with cramped fingers, and tugged at the mess of net covering his hard-nosed face. I pulled and tugged and twisted and untwisted at the unruly knots until little by little the net dropped free of the fish.

"Look out," George shouted, "incoming!" I raised my head just in time to see a dark blurry mass coming straight for me at warp speed. The giant Stellar sea lion plowed through the water, his sleek brown head the size of a basketball. He pushed a rising tidal wave in front of him as he steered a direct path to the boat. His large round eyes glared into mine and I felt a chill down my neck as my role quickly changed from predator to prey. He was closing in fast. His nose was short and fat, tilting upward with a round black cap at the end. His white whiskers stuck out like broom straws on each side of his dark chubby face. The aptly named creature stretched wide his jaws exposing long menacing teeth dripping watery saliva. He let out an enormous roar that blew a gale-force wind in my face. His breath stunk of rotten fish and regurgitated kelp tinged with heaping amounts of other sea garbage. I wanted to puke. Instead, I gripped the fish harder with both hands, terrified, possessive, determined, and shocked into immobility.

Suddenly, I felt a jerk at my neck and tumbled backwards and down to the floor. With lightning speed, George had leapt from the back of the boat, snatched the collar of my jacket and hauled me up and backwards into the boat. He knocked the fish from my hands into the mouth of the sea lion as it rose up to the bow.

It snapped up the tasty morsel and then turned sharply away from the boat, where seconds ago the upper half of my body had dangled over the side with my arms plunged under the frigid water. The metal skiff tipped dangerously back and forth for a while as the waves smashed against the sides from the wake of the huge greedy mammal. I lay in a heap on the floor with slippery slime and red watery blood sloshing around me, mixed with bits of sticky fish scales and sea lice. I felt the beginnings of a new chill as cold water seeped through my jeans.

"Dang, girl. I told you to look out," George huffed between big gulps of air. He sat crumpled up next to me, out of breath from the quick exertion of saving my life from the jaws of the giant sea lion.

Coming around in my mind from terror to reality was slow, but my anger at the loss of the hefty thick salmon I'd had in my hand and had now lost forever to that slimy, slick, slithering thief was starting to take over.

"Well, now what," I screeched. "That salmon would have made us an even twenty-five for the day. Now that sea lion stole him. Now we don't have that fish anymore. Why does he get that salmon when we were out here all morning trying to catch some fish and he has the whole ocean to himself?" I rambled on with this monologue of nonsense until I felt somewhat normal again; all the while George sat still with his arms folded over his chest wearing a look of barely disguised amusement as he waited for me to wind back down. It had been a near miss, but miss all the same. Lucky me.

Stellar sea lions were known to climb aboard fishing boats looking for a handout. They hopped onto lower level diving platforms attached to most boats in hopes of easy pickings. A compassionate angler once tossed a few fish from his boat to a bobbing sea lion and then turned his back. The sea lion whooshed up, grabbed the man by his butt and hauled him overboard. The man smacked him hard on the nose, got free, swam back to the diving platform, and pulled himself back into the boat. He suffered only two minor puncture wounds, a few bruises and a lost wallet.

At one time sea lions numbered in the hundreds of thousands, but they have since declined, perhaps killed off to keep them away or strangled in tangled commercial nets, or maybe just through the normal cycle of life.

One morning in early spring George and I spotted a group of sea lions hiding under the harbor pier, seeming to pause in the water, not swimming in long strides through the channel or bobbing up for the occasional breath of air like submarine telescopes, as they usually did. We had parked the truck at Oscar's Dock and were sitting on a bench facing the channel eating hoagie sandwiches. Moments later, a huge killer whale swooshed up and out of the water, blowing its huge plume of watery air six feet up with a great hiss. Its long body slowly rolled up and over the surface followed by its iconic raised tail dripping cascades of water. The whale disappeared into the ocean again and another great spew came from several yards away as it roamed the area looking for its favorite meal, sea lion. I found myself cheering for the sea lions, willing them to stay hidden for a few more minutes until the gigantic beast moved on to other areas.

This way of life seemed in conflict at times. In an effort to survive in harmony with all the inhabitants of the island I had to shift from one way of thinking to the opposite view as the situation or season dictated. The delicate balance tipped slightly at times, for plants, animals, and humans alike.

I felt a kindred spirit with the majestic spruce trees standing tall all around me like sentinels, protecting me and the other creatures from wind and rain and snow. They brightened the hillsides and valleys with their long bottlebrush needles poking out from rough gray bark. Their constant green branches maintained an artistic balance with the brown and rain-soaked dirt, the straw-colored matted grasses of spring, the pink and purple wildflowers in summer, and red and yellow leaves of alder bushes in the fall. The always-green trees provided a striking contrast against the winter snow, making for a perfect sketch of landscapes in blacks and whites and dark greens. Then we chopped them down for firewood.

I admired the Sitka black-tailed deer as they appeared and disappeared in and out of the bushes scattered across the field behind the house. The small tawny-colored deer nibbled on any piece of bark or limb of alder bush, sometimes pawing away at the chest-deep snow in search of a morsel. I found myself hoping they'd make it through the winter, telepathically encouraging the frail-looking creatures to hang on, keep moving, find something to eat, do whatever they must to survive. I watched them tiptoe around the yard in the spring, munching new bright green shoots of grass, poking up from the slow-thawing ground. They munched contentedly on summer clover and grazed on thick clumps of grasses high enough now to tickle their soft white bellies, growing bigger and stronger as fall rolled around. October was deer season. We shot four that year. Not the ones in my yard, only those living in the specified subsistence areas.

George and I had shouted and laughed at the salmon leaping and splashing in the fresh river water where they strained and struggled against the swift current to complete their mission in the cycle of life. We marveled at their tenacity to venture out into the open ocean at great risk, deftly avoiding the baited hooks and bated breaths of predators. They joyfully returned to their spawning grounds like clockwork, their instinct typically on schedule. May through October we caught them and ate them by baking, smoking, or frying them in scalding hot oil to nourish ourselves.

It seemed to revolve with the seasons, or maybe the natural order of things -this conflict of ideals, balancing, tipping, and balancing again. In one season, one respected, nurtured, and cheered the species on to survival. In the next, one took away. It must be evermore confusing to those who didn't live here.

Recognizing and reconciled to this basic belief in the cycle of life, George and I knew that we too would die, in time. George said to scatter his ashes in front of our cabin, giving himself back to nature, becoming groundcover for the creatures he loved so dearly. Me too, I thought. I will rest on the sandy beach, waiting for the last tide to come in.

7 DELUGE

The sun wasn't up yet as the four men trekked single file down the gangway ladder to the dock below. They hauled backpacks, totes, ice chests, and a variety of firearms along the walkway to the last finger on the pier. The man on board the dull metal cabin cruiser barked orders as soon as they were in sight.

"Where do ya think you're going, on an African safari or something? Where do ya think we're gonna put all that junk? Jaysus, you'd think we were goin' for six months, not six days," Jerry ranted into the darkness. "OK, get that stuff on board and stowed. We're burnin' daylight here." A couple of heads turned upwards, frowning at the still black sky, sprinkled with stars. *Daylight hadn't begun yet—what was he talking about?*

"And a good morning to you, too, Jerry," said George, cheerfully. They had been friends for a few years now and George knew that the best way to get on Jerry's nerves was to be cheerful. Jerry hated cheerful. With the looks and temperament of a grouchy old bear, Jerry was the smartest and most sea-savvy person George had ever had the privilege to sail with. Although they had many scraps and outright arguments between them, George trusted his life to this unsavory character when it came to floating out in the middle of the Gulf of Alaska in any storm, fog, or blizzard Mother Nature happened to throw at them.

George had learned a lot from Jerry over the years, mostly how to survive and navigate the waterways around the island's many inlets and bays, pinpointing certain natural markers such as mountaintops, cliffs, and tree growths. Between the two of them, they had a few narrow escapes from the jaws of death, or the dark depths of the sea. They developed a hard-won mutual respect for each other's talents over the years and when the going got rough, they worked together like a well-oiled motor running in smooth water.

It was hunting season, late October. George deftly hopped over the rail into the 28-foot Wooldridge metal cabin cruiser and turned to assist the others with their gear. It looked like a promising day on the water, and he was just as anxious as Jerry to get the party going. He pushed the hood back on his fleece jacket as he reached for Ted's backpack and rifle. The sky was that peaceful shade of black turning gray as the sun started to roll around the horizon. George's blond hair shone light in the dark cabin and his blue eyes were merry with excitement. George loved being out on the ocean. The sense of freedom, the adventure, and watching nature all around him were the best things about living in Kodiak.

George was friendly and generous, and had a natural curiosity that motivated and inspired his life in many directions. He was also very intense. Underneath the easygoing nature was a keen awareness of his surroundings and the people in it. Growing up in the low-income district of a large city back East, he had learned early in life to be ready to protect and defend. Would-be robbers, thieves, and at least one staff sergeant in the U.S. Air Force had felt the rapid blow of a right hook that could break a nose or jaw with deadly force. He had a low tolerance for fools and sidestepped stupidity with his walk-on attitude. His favorite comment about living in Alaska: "There aren't too many stupid people up here . . . Mother Nature sorts them out."

When the group finished sorting and stowing the gear and settled into their spaces on the boat, George looked at Jerry, waiting for the jerk of his head that meant jump out, untie the line, and cast off. George leapt back into the boat and settled in his own favorite spot, up on the bow, with the wind in his face. From there he could watch the water for deadheads, hidden rocks and reefs, and any other dangers like kelp beds. The October wind was cold and salty and made his eyes water, but he just pulled his hood up and hunkered down with his feet and one arm wrapped around the railing brackets.

They headed out in the light gray dawn, motoring slowly through the channel, past the canneries and warehouses, past the beachfront houses with front yards reaching for the sandy shoreline. George watched sea lions lounging on the rocks lining the opposite side of the channel. They stared back at him with huge round black eyes; one had a scar slanting across his ear, probably from a fight over fish or rock rights, he thought.

George smiled as a bald eagle swerved overhead, dropping with each circle then suddenly diving down and skimming the surface of the water with razor sharp talons. It snatched up a flapping fish with both feet and then lifted upwards in a smooth graceful glide. The eagle headed toward a nearby tree on the shoreline and promptly dropped the fish as he tried to land on the branch. George chuckled as a fast-acting shiny black raven reached the fish first and carted it off into the bushes. With a short angry screech, the eagle launched again, circling over the water.

They cruised past the last channel marker and picked up speed to match the incoming tide as the sturdy boat stepped up to ride the gentle waves. All felt the sense of being free from land and all its limitations. They collectively stared ahead as the first rays of bright sun shone pink and purple in the sky, the water glistened with diamonds scattered as tiny waves rose in the distance. The mirror images of trees and cliffs showed blurry over the flat, calm water as they rounded the bay.

Heading north, they saw a tiny dark speck on the horizon. That was where the boat was heading. Then, north by northwest, they would arrive at Raspberry Island, where they would camp for the next few days for some hunting and fishing. The ocean spread wide and empty to the northeast. No land was visible on the horizon, only the sky meeting the ocean with the slight downward curve on either side of the earth.

Gordon and Ted stood in the back of the boat, one on each side. Both career military men by their obvious straight-back stature and short haircuts, they talked in short sentences and strong tones easily heard above the engine noise as they pointed to sea otters, puffins, and gulls along the way.

Gordon was lean, five feet eleven inches, and straight as a stick with straight black hair and brown eyes. He wore a stern look from years of practice as a master chief in charge of a team of junior enlisted men who worked sixty feet in the air on high voltage power lines. He was quick thinking and always prepared for anything.

Ted walked with a slight bend to his shoulders from his too-tall height of six feet four inches. He had dark brown hair, hazel-specked nervous eyes and his feet were longer than most people's arms. He was arguably the best camp cook this side of the Alaska Range.

Seth could stand straight up and fit under Ted's shoulder. He was small and thin, still wore boy-size pants, but his shirts strained over his oversized arms and shoulders. Like a character out of Popeye, he had massive muscled upper arms from years of rowing boats up and down the Kenai River as a chartered fishing guide. He had a million stories to tell of growing up in wild Alaska, from building a house out of trees to tracking and killing moose with a machete. He knew more about growing and preserving food in Alaska than most published gardeners. He was funny, helpful, and would do anything for a case of beer.

An hour later, Jerry slowed the motor as they rounded a point and headed towards the sandy beach. He steered the boat, riding a wave pushed by the rising tide, straight ahead through the shallow water. He cut the engine and pressed the motor lift button as the bow glided gently onto the black, sandy beach. The men stood aside while Jerry stomped to the stern to check the prop and level of the boat. He made sure it would hold until they off-loaded the gear, and with the rising tide, the boat would be moored back out with an anchor tied to the rocks on shore. They looked at each other, waiting for someone to make the first move.

"Get out!" barked Jerry. At the same time, they all rushed towards the berth, clanging heads and banging shoulders together, cussing and yelling at each other in calamity chaos. "Jaysus," Jerry waved his arms at the bunch. "What a bunch of morons! You all can't fit down there at once, you know! Now start an assembly line and get that stuff outta there!"

Untangling themselves, Gordon and Ted stepped back and sorted themselves out into an assembly line with Seth in the berth. He began handing out totes to Ted; Ted swung the totes to Gordon, who handed them down to George waiting patiently on shore. George made a respectable effort not to laugh, but he could not contain the wide grin. This was going to be a great trip for sure.

The four men started up the beach, each with a load, following Jerry as he turned his head for one more look at the position of his boat. The line was snug and the tide would take care of the rest. Satisfied his boat was secured, he reached the path into the woods and began the hike up the side of the mountain towards the campsite. George brought up the rear. As he marched behind the men, he hummed the song from *The Wizard of Oz* – the part with the marching monkeys - OhREEo, OreOOHHH. Oh. OhREEo. OreOOhhhh. Oh. Gordon and Ted chattered away like two blackbirds and Seth watched the ground, always on the lookout for signs of critters. In another forty-five minutes, they stood at a small clearing. "This is it," said Jerry. "Set up your stuff wherever and we'll take a look around after we eat."

They each selected a spot. George and Seth stretched a tarp over two tree limbs, laid a second tarp on the ground and began putting together their cots. Gordon and Ted set to work constructing their new Cabalas tent, complete with zipper screen door, pounding in stakes at each corner and rolling out the awning attached to a pole on either side.

Jerry eyed the two setups and opted for the Cabalas tent. "I'll just put my stuff in here with you guys. You don't mind, do you?" He stepped through the opening and began rolling out his sleeping bag in one corner. Gordon and Ted looked at each other. "Well, I guess we'll all fit. Gonna be a bit cozy, but at least we'll be warm," Ted said shrugging his shoulders.

Ted started the campfire and pumped up the propane gas grill. His specialty was campfire cooking and homemade bread, although he was known to make excellent salmonberry wine that packed a wallop and still tasted good, maybe too good.

He gently placed the thick steaks across the grill and sliced potatoes and butter onto a sheet of tinfoil, seasoned it with salt and pepper, laid sliced onions on top, rolled the top closed and placed it in the back part of the grill. He opened two cans of beans just enough to let the steam out and set those on the sides. George, Gordon, and Seth came back with arms full of firewood. Seth and George dragged over two logs and Gordon found a third. Jerry watched all this from his camp chair like the royal highness of hunting.

They sat down to a great camp meal, complete with deer meat stew, toasted biscuits and fried jelly pie for dessert. They ate heartily, sat around laughing, and telling jokes, content in the peaceful forest and growing drowsy from full stomachs and all the exercise from the preparations of the day. Quietness came over the camp as the sun slid slowly beyond the mountains and a few birds lingered softly, singing their evening song. In the distance, the rhythmic waves shushed the shore, completing the lush island quiet.

When dusk moved in, it was time to clean up and the four men rose, each setting about some chore that aided in the effort. Jerry, of course, supervised. "Somebody get some water in that bucket, put those pans up outta the way and make sure you don't leave any scraps around. We're gonna have bears all over the place the way you guys clean up. Jaysus holy cripes, I gotta bunch of amateurs around here. Didn't your mothers ever teach you anything?" Jerry chided, pointing vaguely around the circle.

The spell was broken—shattered, more like. The four guys half listened, murmured a few words to each other, and kept doing what they were doing. The pots, pans, utensils, and dishes were washed, dried and hung from a tree limb in a cheesecloth sack and the burnable scraps thrown in the fire. The tin cans were rinsed and put with the tinfoil and other debris into a heavy plastic trash bag, stashed and sealed in the metal lockable container, then moved several yards away from the camp.

Jerry kicked another log onto the fire, sparks shooting up to the now black sky, and said, "Yeah that oughta do it." It was to be assumed that he helped, with that log being rolled in the fire. "Well, I don't know about the rest of ya, but I'm tired. I'm going to bed. Better get some sleep yourselves; we'll be busy tomorrow, that's for sure." He waved an arm at them and disappeared into the tent. The others soon followed. They slept noisily in their various spots, snores competing with grumps and groans and coughs, well into the night. Until the storm hit.

The wind came first, howling through the trees like a freight train, followed by pounding pellets of rain that drenched everything in its path. George sucked in a breath as he heard a loud crash outside his tarp tent. Seth sat up as well and flicked on a flashlight.

"What do you suppose that was, George?" asked Seth through the darkness.

"Don't know, maybe a chair or the picnic table," answered George. Another loud crash and then several shouts made them unclip an opening in the tarp and peer out.

In the silvery night they could just make out Jerry's bulky figure flapping his arms and stomping his feet with all the fury of a scalded cat. They recognized few words in between the expletives and guttural growling coming from across the now smoldering campfire. They listened for a few more seconds, and then Seth turned to George.

"I don't hear anyone else hollering out there, do you?"

"Nope, now that you mention it, that's just Jerry yelling up a storm."

"He's about the only one who would yell back at a storm, that's for sure." Seth chuckled. "What do you think we should do?"

"Let's give him a few more minutes to get it out of himself, and then we'll go see what's up."

A few minutes later, they peered out of their tent. The storm had let up some and the clouds parted just enough to let the moon lift the darkness. Jerry stood at the entrance of the tent, now heavy and sagging with rain. The trees dripped sheets of water as the leaves bent from their burden. The forest grew quiet, ominous, poised and waiting. The heavy rain had soaked the earth, turning it into a mushy mud mixed with flattened mossy lichen, and had destroyed the campfire, scattering charred wood in a watery path down the hill.

Jerry raised his head to the sky. His silhouette standing at the entrance of the tent was dark against the glow from the moon peering down through the trees. His shoulders stuck up stiff, his arms straight down at his sides with clenched fists as he cursed Mother Nature.

Her response was swift and chilling. The roof of the tent could stand no more of its burden and gave way. The front poles snapped, the bulging flap dropped, and six hours of pent up rain dumped on Jerry like a fifty-gallon bucket had tipped on his head.

It happened so suddenly that the others could shout no warning. It slammed into his head and shoulders, rushing down his neck and down his back like Niagara Falls. Jerry was soaked from head to toe in the blink of an eye. For three beats he was silent, his mouth wide open in astonishment as he gasped in a great rush of air.

They saw a giant shiver run the length of his body. Jerry swung around in two full circles with his arms crossed tightly over his chest and his fists stuffed under his armpits. Then he spied the shack between the trees on the far side of their camp.

George and Seth had heard the mumbled voices of Gordon and Ted earlier that night and figured they had found the shack and relocated from the soggy tent. They watched Jerry stomp towards the dilapidated door. He grabbed the wooden latch and shoved it open with a crash. The old hinges, long ago rusted through, finally snapped off and the door fell flat to the floor. The heat rushed up in Jerry's face and the cold swirled around Gordon and Ted.

"Put that door back up," yelled Gordon. "You're letting all the heat out." Gordon and Ted had rigged up kerosene lanterns and emergency paraffin candles inside two silver emergency space blankets draped over a beam. This worked to envelop enough heat to shed their wet clothes and hang them up to dry. Shirts, socks, and jeans were draped across a string running from one nail in the wall to the other side, forming a small cozy area that was warm enough for them to sit comfortably and sip brandy.

Jerry crowded into the small space dripping puddles on the floor but silent, for once. Gordon and Ted eyed each other and shifted over. "Take your wet clothes off, Jerry, you'll warm up faster." Gordon spoke in a more moderate tone as he eyed the shivering, drenched face of his friend.

They each took hold of his jacket and peeled off layer by layer, hanging the various articles along the wall. Ted handed his flask over to Jerry, now huddled in a wool army blanket and sitting on a wooden bench. He took a small sip, and then a big gulp as the shivering slowed.

A half hour later, George and Seth walked in, carefully closing the broken door in place and the group sat together again,
making jovial conversation about their favorite topics: fishing
and hunting. There was no mention of Jerry's defeat at the hands
of Mother Nature, although a few stifled chuckles spilled out
unexpectedly from one or another in the group.

For the next three days, the weather was drizzly, but the wind
was easy, allowing them ample hunting time on the mountain.
When they had filled their allotted deer tags, they packed up the
meat, cleaned up the camp and started for home, a one-hour boat
ride that turned into two days.

About halfway from Anton Larsen Bay, fog rolled in thick
and hovering, masking the way across the open water. It was
a testament to Jerry's instinct and superior navigational skills
when he finally eased the boat into the small Alaska Native village of Ouzinkie. It was a few miles short of their destination,
but a safe mooring place inside a tiny bay away from the choppy,
dangerous straits. They took refuge with the mayor of the village and his round, smiling wife who served them hot coffee
and homemade biscuits with smoked salmon and cheese. They
gathered around an old wooden plank table with hand-hewn
benches, swapping stories of swamped boats and near misses on
the salty, frigid waters.

Two days later the fog lifted and the grateful hunting party
waved goodbye as they set out for home. It had been another
exciting adventure, although somewhat soggy and foggy. The
happy hunters had enough meat for the winter, minus one deer
left with the mayor and his wife for their kind hospitality, which
was typical in the outlying villages.

8 CHECKMATES

It was July of the following year when George and Jerry decided to head out in Jerry's boat to Larsen Bay. As George related much later, it was a strange and scary trip.

They stopped about halfway to the village and camped out on shore. George woke suddenly, blinked several times, and quickly scanned the semi-dark space inside the tent. The distinct smell was in the air. Bear!

Most times you could smell them before you saw them. Pungent, with the scent of wet dog mingled with old socks. He sat up cautiously, quietly pushed back the sleeping bag and slid his feet to the floor. He could hear Jerry snoring in the cot on the other side of the olive green canvas tent. He pulled on his flannel shirt and eased into his pants and boots.

He stood up, undecided what to do next. He could hear the low muffled snort and snuff of the intruder. The bear was close, probably rummaging through the leftovers from the campfire last night. Damn. He should have taken greater care to put everything away. Jerry was a great camp cook, but messy. George pictured the scraps of potato peel Jerry had tossed close to the fire but didn't quite reach the burn area. He remembered too, the one ear of corn still left by the coals. Charred by now, but would still smell good to a bear.

He waited quietly, willing the bear to move on. No such luck. He saw the nose first as it nudged an opening in the flap, letting in a sliver of the light gray dawn, then the brown paw with long, razor-sharp claws poked through the small opening where the snaps attached to the bottom. Suddenly the bear paw jerked forward, the snaps ripped apart and the flap tore open.

"Jerry! Jerry! Bear!" yelled George. Jerry, cut short in mid-snore, jerked back his sleeping bag, jumped up and yelled with the full force of someone who was not at all a morning person.

"Damn, can't a person get any sleep around here? I'm on vacation and the last thing I need is to be woken up at God knows what time it is so early in the morning!"

George had one eye on the bear but was still amazed that someone could wake up so fast and cranky.

Jerry stopped to suck in air for his next rant when he caught sight of the bear, his two front paws inside the tent. "Get out! Get outta here!" Jerry shouted. He picked up his boot and flung it at the bear; it hit the table stacked with pots, pans, plates and ice chest sending it all crashing to the floor with a horrendous clatter and calamity. Most of it flew in the direction of the opening. That was enough for the bear. He turned and ran for the hills, where it was quiet. Jerry turned to George. "What?"

George was speechless, his mind still sorting through the bear scare, the clattering dishes and Jerry yelling like a luna-tic. "Just wanted to let you know about the bear," said George, finally.

"Oh." Jerry blinked once and shrugged his shoulders. "Why didn't you just say so? What time is it? We might as well break camp and get an early start. Don't want to waste the daylight." He plodded over to the mess and picked up his boot.

George turned around before Jerry could see his eyebrows shoot to the top of his head and started rolling up his gear. It was summer in Alaska, meaning nineteen hours of daylight. How can you waste that? George smiled to himself. Jerry was the orneriest man he had ever known, but he was a good friend. He knew more about the Kodiak waters than anyone George knew of and apparently, he could scare off a bear, to boot.

Jerry was gruff and obnoxious, had his own way of doing things, and griped about everything and everybody. On his boat, he was in charge, which meant facing frequent outbursts, including abrasive language and flying objects. Jerry made matters worse by being right most of the time. George didn't question anymore, just obeyed the orders with an inner calm and steadfast allegiance.

Jerry had few friends but George was a compassionate person and learned a lot about running a boat in and around the unpredictable ocean surrounding the island. There were pleasant times as well and George considered it a small price to pay for frequent fishing excursions aboard Jerry's sturdy boat, recently decked out with every piece of emergency gear, sleeping quarters for four, a propane heater, and canned food stuffed in various nooks and crannies.

Jerry had installed a new GPS/Fish Finder on the boat that showed tiny pictures of fish swimming near the boat, as well as how deep the water was and which direction the boat was going. He could plot different points on the screen and store them in its memory. Although this worked well as a backup, George would still rather rely on Jerry's knowledge and experience. It got them safely through more than one disaster.

Good equipment was handy to have, but total reliance on it was asking for trouble. He knew of such cases where other boats ran aground, ended up somewhere else because of a glitch in the data point entries, or shorted wiring on the boat. Even a compass used in Alaska was going to be off a few degrees.

Jerry's temper seemed spent on his vigorous wakeup, so things were looking good. They finished rolling up their sleeping bags with extra pants, shirts, and socks tucked inside, stuffed them in waterproof carryalls, stowed the pans, plates, and silverware in a plastic container and repacked the ice chest. They carried everything down to the boat and pushed off as the tide reached high at three-plus feet. The boat motored smoothly through calm seas and sliced its way south, heading for Larsen Bay.

Some of the best halibut and salmon fishing grounds lay in and around these protected waters on the south end of Kodiak. Larsen Bay was one of six villages settled around the edges of the island tucked into various bays and lagoons. The only access was by boat or small aircraft. Some villages had dirt runways; others required a seaplane to get there.

Larsen Bay was one of the largest, with about 150 residents year round, swelling to 300 during the summers. Its population was mostly Native Alaskans with a sprinkling of Norwegians, Russians, and Irish that worked in the fish cannery during the summers. The village had a school with two teachers who taught all grades to about thirty children living there. The teachers were provided housing and a stipend as well as paid college tuition for a four-year commitment. Some enjoyed the quiet, rugged lifestyle and stayed for years, others quit after the first few days.

Larsen Bay canneries 2006

There was no store, no theater and no live entertainment, except what the residence made for themselves. They lived simple lives. Some worked for the Kodiak Alaska Native Association and kept the village operating, such as the "Village Public Safety Officer," "mail person," "snow removal person," or "mechanic." Most owned fishing sites or worked in the cannery during the summer seasons.

"Ahoy there, mates," called Roger from the shore. "You're here early. I figured you'd get here this afternoon."

George tossed Roger the line to tie the boat to a cleat on the dock and shouted back. "We had an alarm clock of sorts that woke us earlier than we expected." He grinned at Roger as he set out the two buoys along the front and back sides of the boat to sandwich between the dock and the boat.

"Yeah, an early alarm clock alright," growled Jerry. "George started yelling in my ear for some stupid reason at four a.m. this morning. Can't get any sleep with him around that's for sure." Jerry flipped the switch to raise the engine out of the water, and then shut off the electronics and batteries.

George shrugged. "Just trying to let you know a big bear was coming in the tent to kiss you good mornin', that's all."

"A cub, you mean. That thing was no bigger than a small dog. Don't know what all the fuss was about. Hey Roger, get that ice chest over there and grab those two bags over here while you are at it," barked Jerry.

Roger stepped into the boat, grabbed the two packs, and lifted one end of the ice chest. "Good morning to you too, Jerry." He knew Jerry well and countered his orneriness with a sense of humor that was always contagious.

"Yeah well, what's so good about it anyway," scowled Jerry.

George gripped one end of the ice chest with Roger on the other, hefted his backpack, stepped off the boat in sync with Roger and walked up the old, waterlogged dock. Balancing the load between them, they walked down the wide dirt path leading to the house.

"Should be a great weekend for fishing," said Roger.

"Yep, looking forward to catching some butt," answered George. "How goes it with you, Roger?"

"Fine, George, just fine. If it got any better I couldn't stand it," was Roger's friendly response. They set the ice chest, bags, and backpacks inside the screened porch, clasped each other in a quick backslapping man-hug and walked back down to the dock. Jerry began busily moving things around on the boat, making useless racket, as he spied them coming.

"'Bout time you guys came back. I can't carry all this stuff by myself, you know." George and Roger reached for Jerry's backpack, boots, and fishing rods, and stood back as Jerry stepped onto the dock. They watched him stomp over the worn wooden planks, stumble on an uneven board, straighten himself upright and walk on.

"When you gonna fix this dilapidated piece of junk, Roger," Jerry griped over his shoulder as he clambered off the dock and made his way up the dirt path. "A person could kill himself just comin' to see you. Been catchin' any fish in these here waters? And I don't mean those minnows like last time, I mean some real fish." Roger grinned at George as they caught up behind Jerry.

"We got some real whoppers for ya Jerry, just waiting for you to catch 'em," quipped Roger.

"Oh, and I suppose I gotta catch all the fish now too, is that it?" He grumbled up the steps and into the house. George and Roger looked at each other in silent amusement. Yep, it was going to be a great weekend.

They had settled into their bunks for the night, Jerry already asleep, when the phone call came. George could hear Roger in the other room talking on his radio receiver.

"Got it Nick, over at the Petersons' house. I'll be right there." George walked into the living room as Roger pulled on his VPSO jacket and snapped pepper spray to his belt.

"I'll be back in a while. Gotta go get Summers out of Jack Peterson's house. Drunk and disorderly as usual," said Roger as he picked up his keys and slipped a small flashlight into his jacket pocket.

"Need some help?" George offered, noticing the grim look on Roger's face.

"Nah, I got this one covered. Thanks, man." Roger was the Village Public Safety Officer, born and raised in Larsen Bay, and he knew everyone and everyone's business. Most of the difficulties involved alcohol abuse, and some situations got ugly, but he handled them with calm efficiency.

Roger was six feet two inches with smooth black hair worn slightly over his collar and dark brown eyes that crinkled at the corners when he smiled. At thirty-five years old he was lean and well built, if a bit weathered, and possessed an inner strength and self-confidence that made people notice when he walked into a room. His easygoing manner switched to command-and-control cop in an instant, taking charge of a situation with swift action and sound judgment. He also had a knack for reading people, as well as animals, which aided immensely in bringing calm to chaos, whether it required breaking up fights or removing unwanted bears or unwelcome residents from houses, driveways, or tool sheds.

Some of the residents were relatives, others friends, and some bears were bigger than others, but animals and humans alike had come to respect Roger's authority and went on their way with only mild resistance. Others required immediate action, and on rare occasions, he called for backup by means of the Alaska State Troopers. However, the logistics of being thirty flight minutes away or an hour and a half by boat meant the problem was usually resolved by Roger and his assistant, or was beyond anyone's help, except for the coroner's or the Fish and Game wardens.

Cannery workers, who swarmed in during the summer fishing season, brought a handful of problems for the VPSO and his assistant. The language barrier made things more difficult and their tendency to be fearful of any authority made for a fight waiting to happen. Other times it was careless tourists or neighbors disputing over something stupid, with alcohol a strong contributing factor. That time it was two best friends heavily inebriated and having it out.

Roger pushed open the door, grabbed both young men by their shirtfronts and pulled them together. Their heads cracked hard against each other and when they both stumbled backwards from the impact, Roger handcuffed both before they knew what had happened.

Ben, Roger's assistant, took one by the arm and Roger took the other. They pulled them out of the house and helped them into the police vehicle. At the station, located a hundred yards farther down the dirt road, Ben locked each one in a holding cell, locked the doors, and hung the keys on the wall.

"I'll watch 'em tonight, Ben. Come and get me in the morning," Roger said as he waved him off, and then made himself comfortable in his tilt-back desk chair.

At seven the next morning, it was clear and calm outside and the sun was already up past the distant hills, promising a great day for fishing. Roger opened the front door, walked into the house and found Jerry sitting in his recliner with a mug of coffee in hand and his feet propped up on the coffee table. George was in the kitchen setting the table for breakfast.

"Where have you been? You look like something the cat dragged in," mumbled Jerry.

Roger slipped off his jacket, hooked it on the nail by the door and toed off his boots.

"Oh, just a bit of a ruckus down the road last night. No biggie," Roger answered cheerfully, back to his easygoing mode. "Say, that coffee smells good."

"Yeah, not bad. I could use a warm-up since you're headin' that way," Jerry said, holding out his mug.

"Sure, Jerry, be right back." Roger stepped into the kitchen carrying Jerry's empty mug. George handed him his own mug already filled with fresh coffee.

"Have a seat. These eggs will be ready in a minute." He took Jerry's mug from Roger, filled it up and set it down on the table in front of the opposite chair.

"Yo Jerry. Your coffee's out here, come on out," called George. He flipped three eggs over easy onto the plate, stabbed three sausages, added them to the plate and set it down as Jerry sauntered into the kitchen.

"Smells eatable, anyway. This mine?" He sat down in front of the plate, grabbed the fork and started in.

"Guess so," mumbled George, turning back to the stove. He set down another plate for Roger, fixed one for himself and refilled coffee cups all around. They finished eating, cleaned up, and started out the door, happy to be on the way to enjoy a beautiful day.

"We'll go out to the point first to catch some bait. I'm all out," Roger said as he steered the boat away from the dock and out towards a treeless ridge that sloped gently down to the shore in a wide sweep of green grass and alder bushes, then abruptly broke off at the end.

"You mean we have to catch fish to catch fish?" grumbled Jerry. "Well, fine let's get at it then." Roger slacked off on the engine as they neared the shallows in the lagoon then turned it off as the boat slowly glided through the flat water.

"Where's my rod?" Jerry barked as he spied his rod, grabbed it down from the overhead rack and stomped to the rear of the boat. George and Roger sat still, giving him room to get situated. Jerry unhooked the leader, pulled out a yard of line from the reel, grabbed the tackle box and flipped it open in one brisk motion. With all the deftness of a surgeon, he tied on the set of six tiny hooks spread apart by three or four inches of light line, and connected it to a swivel that was clipped to the main line. He tossed the whole setup over the side just as the boat was settling in the water.

With the first jerk of the line, he now had a look of pure joy on his face. Fishing was what he lived for and no one could match his expertise and flair. George and Roger stood back, fiddling a bit with their gear, not wanting to interrupt this rare moment. Then they dropped their lines in the water, too.

All was silent as they concentrated on catching the seven-inch silvery herring. Within in minutes, all three men were pulling in four or five fish at a time, tossing them in the bucket and dropping lines again. It was intense and exciting activity as they dropped the hooks down, waited for a count of three as the small fish bit the hooks, and then jerked them up and into the boat.

A huge school of fish swarmed around the boat just under the water like a black cloud of buzzing bees irritated at the intrusion. Whooping and hollering, the men dropped their lines again and again, and then pulled them up quickly as the angry herring bit the hooks in a frenzy. The three of them scrambled around the deck, bumping into each other, getting slimed up, soaked down, and having a blast as swinging rods, hooks, and lines whipped through the air, around to the bucket, and back into the water. In no time, the buckets were full.

"That's enough, you guys, we have two buckets here. This will get us by," Roger said as he shook the last two herring off the tiny hooks. George and Jerry reeled in their lines, unhooked the herring sets, dropped them in the tackle box, and propped the rods into the rod holders. George hopped up onto the bow and hauled up the anchor. One hand after the other, he pulled it up, coiling the line into a neat basket, and set the anchor on the mat, then hopped back down into the cabin. Roger turned on the engine and the boat plowed through the incoming tide back out to the bay. Perfect timing, for sure. As the old saying went, incoming tide, incoming fish. Jerry caught the first big halibut, followed by two for George and another for Roger. A great day on the water, they all agreed.

Back on shore, Jerry plopped the biggest halibut down on the plywood table and filleted the first side before Roger and George got their knives out. "I'll get this one," barked Jerry, slicing away with practiced flair. "You two work on those minnows you caught. I would have thrown 'em back if I were you. Downright embarrassing, if ya ask me." He actually had a grin on his face as he glanced up at the other two. They knew this was Jerry's favorite activity and nobody could do it better. The men commenced with jovial bantering, jibing each other about the size of various things until the last fish was fillet.

They wrapped and stacked the fish in the freezer, cleaned up, changed clothes, and headed for the local café, ravenous after a great day of fishing. Fishing in Kodiak was an intense physical workout. It was hard work, but the joy of the catch, the day on the water and the camaraderie amongst good friends made it all worthwhile.

It was late in the evening, though the sun was still high in the sky, and the café was crowded with all the locals and cannery workers just off their second shift.

Roger stepped in, made a quick glance around without moving his head and took in the situation with long practiced-experience. The place was rowdy and people were tipsy already. He walked slowly through the middle of the crowd with his special air of calm assertiveness, catching the eye of the rowdies. The atmosphere instantly relaxed from angry shouting and tension to friendly chatter and laughter. Roger had that effect on people. He had a funny story or a pleasant comment for everyone he met and a serious look when the situation called for it; most important, he had compassion for those who didn't have it so easy, yet chose to stay here and keep the village culture alive.

Roger had left the village a couple of times years ago, looking for something beyond this simple rural life, but he would come back each time like a salmon returned to its birthplace. This basic way of life and the people who struggled to survive here always pulled him back to what he felt was important. The village lifestyle demanded resourcefulness, creativity, and basic survival instincts against the frigid dark winters and busy, long days of summer.

Two people stood up and hailed Roger over. "Hey Roger, come and sit down, we're done here. How'd it go on the water?"

"A fair day, Daniel, thanks," answered Roger, shaking hands with the two Native Alaskans. George and Jerry pulled out the wooden ladder-backed chairs, worn smooth from years of use, and sat down at the sturdy picnic-type table set with red checked placemats and silverware rolled in white paper napkins. The place was rustic but clean, and run by an Alaskan Native named Jack Malutin. He was a large, burly man with thick black hair covering his head, neck, and most of his face and round black eyes that gave him the appearance of a giant panda bear. He nodded at Roger from behind the bar, then caught Renee's eye and cocked his head in their direction.

Renee was the only server in the place and had years of experience dealing with the bar crowds. She took in the two newcomers sitting with Roger with a swift look up and down, pulled out her small pad and pressed down the pen top. "What will you have, people?"

Her polite but no-nonsense, make-it-quick temperament did not sit well with some, but she was efficient, attentive, and had a memory like a steel trap. She was thirty-four, average size, with light brown hair pulled back in a braided ponytail and large navy blue eyes that missed nothing. More observant than most, she picked up on nonverbal talk and sensed vibes from people and responded accordingly. The good vibes were coming from Roger and George - that left the bad vibes coming from Jerry. She zeroed in on the negativity like a bullet to the bull's eye.

"What do you have that's any good?" Jerry growled as he plopped his elbows on the table and stared at her not unpleasant face.

"It's all good mister, else you wouldn't be here, would ya?" she countered.

"Not like there's any other choice around here that I can see," Jerry threw back.

"That's exactly right." She paused for effect. "So. Let's start again, shall we?" Renee glared at Jerry. "What will you have?" Silenced for a count of three beats, Jerry's mouth was working but no counter snide came out. He swiveled his eyes over to Roger for a quick diversion.

"What are you getting that's any good, Roger?" Jerry asked. Roger looked up at Renee with a barely hidden grin and a twinkle in his eyes. He said he'd have the bear burger, fries and coffee. George ordered the halibut sandwich, coleslaw, and Coke. Three heads swiveled to Jerry.

"Guess I'll have to order something on this greasy—"

Before he could finish, Renee leapt on that with a firm "No you don't! As I said, mister, if you don't like it, go somewhere else."

They locked eyes like two bulls in a pen for a full minute. The tension was thick, the challenging stares battled against each other like a ping-pong of fury flying back and forth. Then she blinked slowly. It broke the tension. She resumed her most courteous posture and held her pen expectantly over her note-pad. To the bewilderment of George and Roger, Jerry politely asked for a bear burger, fries, and Coke. Renee scribbled on her pad, abruptly turned, and walked to the kitchen.

Jerry followed her all the way with his eyes, wearing a look of pure astonishment. Then a host of other emotions marched across his face one by one. First shock, then fury, then came the "nerve of her" glare, then came something altogether different from what either Roger or George had seen before. They looked at each other in confusion.

Later that night after Jerry went to bed, George and Roger agreed. It had been a strange encounter. Scary, almost. The sparks between those two sent chills up and down the spine. It was getting embarrassing, too.

Surprising both of them, Jerry announced the next morning that he wanted to stay a few more days. Ah, the value of a good mate. In a place where survival was most important, a good mate was essential. Whether onboard a fishing boat or landlocked on this remote piece of rock, it took teamwork to get by—the struggles were halved and the rewards doubled.

Thus, a relationship blossomed between this unlikely pair. They seemed to match each other perfectly. Gruff exteriors had met glare for glare, fueled by a similar passion for plowing through life head-on and knocking insipidness away like small flies. They both possessed a forceful strength of character tempered by barely civilized manners and a deeper compassion, carefully masked to protect themselves from despised frivolity and superficial niceties. Time and friendly sparring moved Jerry and Renee ever closer together like two glaciers calving into the sea of love.

George and Jerry finally waved goodbye to Roger as he untied the line to the boat and tossed it over the bow. George and Jerry made several trips back to this unique fishing village, with its colorful characters and simple but difficult way of life. Whenever George mentioned this bizarre love story with unabashed incredulity, I was elated and secretly affirmed what I thought Jerry had needed for a long time now: a likewise mate.

George and I shared some great times with Roger through the years and sadly watched as he married and divorced three times and still kept looking for that special someone to share his life in the village. Larsen Bay appeared to be a charming place at first and Roger made a gallant effort each time to make his chosen one feel comfortable and content, but alas, the rugged, deprived lifestyle soon overpowered the charm and one by one, they had left him.

The remote village life did not suit most outsiders. It was an exciting place to visit, full of adventure, and the freedom to do as you pleased without the stress and demands of big-city life. George had said one day after a hectic week, "We should move to Larsen Bay, shouldn't we?" We considered living there for a while, but soon decided we were remote enough. Like most of the remote villages tucked in around small bays and lagoons on

Kodiak Island, there were even fewer resources, even for the basics like grocery stores and hardware stores. The people worked together, shared the fish bounty in the summer, and huddled together to keep each other entertained in the winter.

Mostly, what kept Roger and the others permanently attached to the village, were the people and the lifestyle. It was a challenge to get along sometimes, but these were people deeply involved with each other, through good and bad, scary and sad. And, occasionally they won with Mother Nature, and continued to maintain the village culture.

9 THE CHALLENGE

Learning to coexist and share food with the largest brown bears in the world was a daunting task. We were forced to develop a vigilance and keen sense of awareness, along with nerves of steel, previously undeveloped while living in heavily populated concrete-clad cities.

It took time and practice to learn how to listen to the distinct sounds and recognize the smells around us and at the same time pursue the coveted salmon from the rivers for our winter food supply. Roughly, three thousand five hundred bears inhabited the island. We soon discovered that these longtime residents already claimed our favorite fishing holes and they had their own perspective on life.

Hungry Bear

It was an early brisk fall morning when the bear sauntered down the well-worn path to the river for his breakfast. He intended to feast on fresh salmon, same as yesterday and the day before and the day before that. Halfway down, the dark brown bear stopped dead in his tracks, his sharp nose already picking up the scent. His ears prickled at the disturbing noise.

The smell and sounds were unmistakable. Imprinted in his mind since birth, he instinctively grew cautious and wary. Fishing in his favorite spot were two humans. If they had been other bears or any other creatures, there would have been no hesitation. But humans were unpredictable. The bear knew from experience what the consequences could be. Still, he was a creature of habit and he was hungry.

It was the best spot on the river that snaked down to a wide beach of black sand striped with white, formed from the rock particles eroded from the volcanoes that formed the island. The beach was crescent shaped with rocks and boulders stacked up on each side, long ago fallen from the cliffs above. The waves slid in at an angle, crossing the mouth of the skinny river and slipping around the smaller rocks to make a deep pool of calm water at one end of the shoreline.

Here the fish congregated, stacked together side by side, swaying slowly in the smooth, glassy water. It was easy pickings—just a plunge downward with two thick, heavy front paws with sharp claws. Then it was just a matter of sticking his big furry head into the water, grabbing the fish in his large carnivorous jaws and rising up with his catch.

After eight or ten fish, he could rest on the warm, soft sand, lay his head on his huge furry paws and nap away the afternoon. He had envisioned such a day since awaking this morning, but there they were. Humans.

The bear stopped behind an alder bush and watched the humans with wary interest. At first, he was angry. This was *his* spot. This was his beach and his river and his fish. Suddenly his nose picked up his favorite scent: salmon. He padded quietly over to another bush where the smell was stronger and spotted the fish lying on the bank just back from the river.

He glanced first at the anglers, and then eyed the three tasty fish still flopping on the sand. The grit was sticking to their gills and along their shiny silver scales. Small particles danced up each time the tails and heads flopped up and down on the beach. The fish were right there, just a few yards away. Flopping and flopping. The bear looked back at the anglers.

George and I stood at the edge of the river silently fishing. Long fiberglass rods extended out over the water, lines taut, dipping down, and disappearing into the water. With small jerky motions, the pink metal lures in the shape of miniature fish moved through the current, enticing the salmon to bite. We didn't talk. We focused intensely on the motion of the lure and the feel of the rubber-gripped handles of our rods so as not to miss a bite.

Slowly we cranked the reels with the small levers attached to the winding spools. With each turn, we were silently sending messages across the water: "Bite, fish! Come on, bite!" The line twirled back onto the reel, inches at a time, slowly pulling the lure back to the rod.

As the lure neared his boots, George raised the rod, clicked the button, swung it up and back over his shoulder then swiftly hurled his arm forward. The rod snapped forward, the line followed. The lure sailed through the air and dropped into the river with a splat. He let it sink for a count of three, and then began turning the lever again, slowly. He stared out at the school of fish, dorsal fins visible above the sparkling water as the fish moved in unison against the current.

Splash! SPLASH! A salmon jumped out of the water just yards in front me. "Dang! Did you see that one, George?" I quickly reeled in the rest of my line, jerked the rod up, back, and forward again, aiming the lure at the ripples where the salmon had just jumped. I silently counted to three, and then turned the lever, slowly, slowly, concentrating hard. George didn't answer, deep in concentration himself, hoping to catch the next one.

The bear, unable to contain his hunger any longer, moved in. He was an old bear, and had learned the hard way to be cautious of humans. Though smaller by more than half his size, they could kill. Swiftly, with firepower meant for an elephant, humans had many times taken down a bear before he could react. He looked again at the flopping fish, then over to the unwary humans. His caution gave way to his empty stomach.

He moved with amazing stealth for an animal his size and silently reached the salmon. His jaws clamped down on the nearest fish and he quickly moved back behind the alder bush. With hungry determination, he ripped off the head and chewed. Holding down the tail with knife-sharp claws, he bit off the front half of the fish, chewed, swallowed, and then chomped down the last half.

His lips and chin were tinged red with fish blood. He looked up at the anglers again. They continued to swing the rods, up, back, forward, up, back, forward, unaware of his presence. He moved to the second fish. His jaws clamped down on it and he turned and quietly moved back to the alder. He quickly ate the fish, leaving only a trace of blood and scales on the sand.

Far from satiated, he looked once more at the anglers. One fish still lay on the beach, flopping slightly, slowly succumbing to the inevitable. A few steps more and he would reach it.

SQUAWK! SQUAWK! The large black raven shouted his noisy warning as he flew low through the air, aiming at the bear. SQUAWK! Startled by the sudden noise of the bird, George and I whirled around to the beach. The bear jerked his head up at the same time.

Time stopped, the air was silent, the world stood still, as we stood face to face with the bear. Strangely, my thoughts ran philosophical.

Humans and bears encountered each other with primal fear, first. It had been learned through centuries that man and beast must fight it out. One must overpower the other. One species must try to dominate. One must rule, the other must submit, disappear, or die. Who would decide? Who would make the first move? Was the script already written? Was the outcome in stone? No way.

There were three, not two, possible outcomes in any encounter between two forces, or species. There was always the ending that was not a fight to the death. It was the drama of many stories, sensationalized where a fight to the death was expected. However, there were just as many stories where the outcome was mutually satisfactory.

George and I slowly lowered our rods, preparing to grab and shoot our inadequate pistols or turn and dive into the icy river. The bear lowered his head and watched us. Both sides were cautious, fearful, wary, and weighing the chances of winning against the consequences of losing. Then the bear daringly moved to the last fish, gently lifted it in his red-rimmed jaws and stepped sideways, keeping his eyes firmly on us. He moved toward the path and kept on going out of sight.

The moment was brilliant, like a flash of clear crystal light, a sunray parting the clouds. The challenge was spectacular. The outcome was most satisfying. The drama was there, the first instinct of fear slowly changed to wary respect. No catastrophe, no wounds or scars, no death. Humans could coexist with bears with one premise: we were not at the top of the food chain out here, so we couldn't be greedy. We had many occasions during frequent trips into bear country, to test that new theory of ours.

10 RURAL AWAKENING

It was August 1996 when we came home to find another notice tacked to our door. Apparently, the landowners had decided to build another housing development on the mobile home park site. We would all have to vacate the premises—in ninety days.

One by one, entire households were dragged away by large flatbed tow trucks. Disconnected water pipes, electrical wiring, and phone lines lay dead and scattered on the ground. A giant earthmover poised menacingly at the end of the park, ready to demolish the once carefully tended lots, now mere outlines of lives in neat rectangles. The site was bulldozed and rebuilt with fancy, noisy neighborhoods of lookalike housing units, complete with paved roads, driveways and squared-off playgrounds with brightly colored swings and sliding boards.

A few residents sold out and moved to apartments, others found small lots close to town on which to perch their homes. George and I moved to the rural part of Kodiak, about ten miles outside the city limits in a sparsely populated woodsy area called Monashka Bay. We found a two-acre lot, thick with spruce trees, alder bushes, salmonberry bushes, and wild strawberry patches, close to the top of a mountain.

On the day of the move, we watched with mixed excitement and terror as the heavy-duty tow truck, pulling everything we owned, crawled slowly up the rocky, steep hill, grinding gears and spitting great black puffs of exhaust. It pulled farther up the hill and then backed down carefully into the gravel driveway and onto the rectangular space George had outlined in pink surveyor's tape.

The workers unhitched the mobile home from the truck, blocked up the four corners of the steel frame, leveled it up and waved off. We worked the thin metal skirting back in place, rearranged the inside, and we were in. Or so we thought.

We sat on a tree stump sipping coffee and appreciating the quiet sounds of nature. Birds tweeted and eagles flapped overhead, squirrels chattered, and a few dogs barked a welcome in the distance. However, no people were there, no vehicles roared to life, no traffic zipped by on the gritty dirt road. We were the only residents up there at the time. The seldom-traveled dirt road continued up and over a smaller hill and then came to a dead end.

"We'll be in no danger of a tsunami up here," George said as he pointed to the ribbon of deep blue ocean far below us. "Look at the view!" Indeed, we glimpsed patches of shimmering blue bay between the tall Sitka spruce trees to the east. We spotted two other houses in the distance, tucked between clumps of trees, with pieces of roof or corners of weathered siding visible from where we stood looking south. The north offered another view of the ocean and Spruce Island, green and shapely, rising up from her depths with a few smaller islands like shadows floating on the horizon between the ocean and the sky. To the west, the mountain continued up to the sky, its trees marching along in various stages of height until the very tips of those on the top became shrublike.

George and I took long walks in the fields and woods surrounding the property, exploring our new and picturesque piece of the rock. Blackie and Nightmare trotted along, happily sniffing the trees and bushes heavy with other animal scents. We laughed as squirrels scolded us and marveled as glossy black ravens floated above, wings almost touching one another, zigzagging across the dusky sky in perfect sync.

One calm evening, in the waning light of a fall sunset, we sauntered down a dirt path to a small clump of trees in the far corner of our property. George made a tiny campfire and we sat on the soft spongy lichen roasting hot dogs and eagerly talking of next year's plans. It was a treasured moment of simplicity and joy, similar to a moment we had shared more than twenty-five years before and over three thousand miles away, in a much different place. I was perplexed by this connection. While we seemed to have come a long way, nothing had changed, really. Or had it?

We now lived outside the city limits, beyond state road maintenance and snowplows and mail delivery and streetlights. The winters up there were even more frigid, the winds howled louder and the snow piled higher and stayed on the ground longer. The steep dirt road was choked with snow and ice for days at a time in the winters and spattered with teeth-chattering potholes in the summers. We wore miners' lights to walk the dogs, get to the truck, or shovel snow, and used a blowtorch to thaw out the constantly freezing water pipes beneath the trailer. The property included a 250-foot-deep water well in the front and a 1,200-gallon septic tank buried in the back field.

We diligently wrapped the water pipes securely with insulation and heat tape, as recommended by a friend, stockpiled several cords of wood until our backs adamantly refused to do more, and stacked the cupboards with canned goods, dog food, and water jugs. The local power company hooked up the electricity a few days later. We thought we were ready for anything. However, the last twelve years of cushiony "city life" had done little to prepare us for life in the most rural part of this already remote land.

It was deep into winter, our first one on the hill, when a vicious blizzard slammed into the island and lingered for days. It was dark and stormy, the kind of weather where snow blasted sideways past the windows with eighty-knot winds gusting and whipping and blowing hard and fierce. Huge white snowdrifts had already reached five feet up the sides of the trailer and clogged in the driveway. It piled upwards in sculptures of white, leaving vague mounded images where once lay bushes, small trees, and our truck.

George and I huddled at our kitchen table, staring into the flickering dim glow of a kerosene lamp. The aged and groaning diesel-fed furnace finally died and we had used the last of our firewood a week before. The power had gone out, taking with it the lights, stove, and phone, and with no heat source, the water pipes were frozen solid. I tipped the last bottle of our water supply into the coffeepot and watched it brew, slowly dripping the brown liquid into the pot, hoping we'd have enough propane to finish it up.

George wasn't saying much, not unusual, since sometimes he didn't say anything for long spurts of time, and then when he did open up, out flowed brilliant ideas and theories. Not about building a rocket or saving the world (although he had great ideas about that) or politics and things gone wrong that could be made right with the federal government. George had great ideas that were basic and useful - like how to survive and live off the land and use what was at hand; Brilliant ways to make campfires with a piece of twine and one match, cook salmon into savory meals on a flattened coffee can, and carve deer into choice cuts with a pocketknife. Some were innovative engineering feats, like standing up a 32-foot wood framed wall using our pickup truck, and lifting heavy logs from the deep ravine using a block and tackle slung over a tree. I eagerly encouraged his ideas and willingly followed along as an apprentice to this new way of life.

George sat there in eerie silence. I wanted to tell him that Kodiak was the perfect place for those great ideas, and the perfect place for us. I felt the gloomy mood that had settled over George drifting towards me. I waved my gloved hand at the air trying to ward off the dreaded suffocating presence that hung so thick around us.

I did not want to leave. Not again. Not from this place either. Somewhere along the way, I had come to appreciate that mystical island, its rugged beauty, nature, trees, animals, eagles and yes, rainstorms and snowstorms as well. Of course, we had lived in town up until then. This was a tad different. Still, this had become my dream as well as George's. He wanted to live like Daniel Boone in the wilderness in Kentucky. This was not Kentucky, but it was definitely wilderness.

I wanted to stay. I wanted to help George make his dreams come true. All it took was hard work, we'd both agreed, back on that sunny summer day as they pulled the trailer onto the spot George had lined out with pink tape. It seemed a different place now. Little had I known.

I poured the last cup of hot coffee in George's cup, stirred in the mountains of cream and sugar, just the way he liked it, and slid the cup over in front of him so the steam would warm his face. He gripped the cup with icy hands, poking out from inside the heavy parka, and muttered a "thanks."

I stepped around to the back of his chair and softly kneaded the stiffened muscles along his shoulders and neck. The skin was tight, the muscles taut with worry and stress. I tried to think of some way to help. I felt like we were teetering on the edge, too close to quitting.

Nothing would break George more than feeling like he failed. It was not his fault, of course. Neither of us had had any idea what we were getting into. In other places, it didn't take much to figure out the daily routines. In the big cities, it was easy find the directions for the commute to work, or the best times to avoid the rush-hour traffic, or when to go to the store to avoid the crowds, or where to locate a good technician to fix the truck. However, this was different.

The problems were new, the solutions tough to understand. How much wood was needed for the winter? We had thought seven trees and a mountain of split wood would be enough. How could we contend with no power? If it was an electrical problem in the house, George would have fixed it long ago, but the problem was at the source. Downed power lines were not something that he could just walk out there and fix. And we hadn't thought about the heat tape becoming useless without power. We had so diligently wrapped each section of heat tape around the entire line of pipes, start to finish, careful not to leave any gaps that could freeze. Of course, the heat tape only worked if electricity ran through it.

We had thought of propane for the coffeepot and kerosene lamps and flashlights with batteries, but had not prepared for frozen pipes, no heat, and no electricity. It was a constant battle. As soon as we figured out one thing, another popped up that we hadn't thought of. It was enough to tamp down even the best of pioneering spirits.

In a sudden flash, I decided we were not yet defeated—not yet. We just couldn't be. We had been through so much already to get this far. We just needed to hang on a little longer. Just maintain, keep a little spark glowing for now, and then all would be well. Just a spark.

To George, it was not a question of what happened, good or bad, right or wrong. It was that some effort was made to fix it. A hard effort was worth any failure. The trick was to keep at it. Failure by our definition didn't exist unless you quit. Setbacks, as we tended to feel about most disappointments and trouble we had heretofore encountered, were to be expected. Everyone knew setbacks, if they had lived at all. Setbacks just meant you stepped back and thought the process through and tackled it again.

My mind raced wildly, explaining all this to George in silence, as I knew he would not be receptive to any conversation at that moment. I looked around the trailer trying in my mind to find an answer, anything that would be useful for something, while I continued to knead George's shoulders through the thick parka.

My eyes moved slowly past the coffee cups dangling from hooks twisted into the wall, past a small grouping of pictures, of family, mostly, past the curtains that I had made from cut-up pillowcases, too flimsy, I realized, as they billowed slightly at the window's edge from the icy drafts spewing into the room.

My eyes suddenly snapped back to the group of pictures. There were six small ones and two very large ones—all framed in wood. I mentally spotted three more in the bedroom. My eyes darted back to the kitchen counter where the phonebook lay. Nice thin pages that would wad up easily. It was only about a quarter inch thick—Kodiak didn't have many residents or businesses back then—but it would be enough, I thought, with growing excitement.

I stepped into the living room and reached for two of the smaller frames. The first was a family picture, of George's family, a family gathering ten years ago with everyone smiling at the camera with plastic pasted-on expressions not quite reaching their eyes. It was the last photo taken after the funeral of George's mother. His father was in the center of the professional photograph surrounded by his six children, including George. The next frame held a picture I had taken of my brother and sister at his house back when I visited them in Pennsylvania three years ago. It was a perfect June day, I remembered. I fought down the pang of longing, sharp in my chest, to be there instead of here.

I quickly flipped the pictures over and pulled up the fasteners, lifted out the backs and the pictures and then the glass, carefully placing them on top of the coffee table. I did the same with two other small pictures, one of a beautiful red fox, the other a huge coffee-colored brown bear taken last summer on the river near our favorite fishing hole.

I smacked the wooden frames against the edge of the table one by one until they lay in broken pieces on the floor, then carried them to the woodstove and set them on the floor next to the phonebook. I glanced sadly back at the precious glossy pictures. They would need to perish as well, but not until the phonebook pages ran out. I suddenly wished Kodiak had a lot more residents.

I stood in front of the largest frame, strategically placed on the far wall, a dramatic painting of colorful ducks flying low over a reedy autumn marsh with two black Labradors running in eager pursuit. It captured a perfect moment where the satiny dog's ears were flipped up behind their heads, tails straight out, paws stretched out front and back and long pink tongues whipped to the side of their happy faces. The frame was solid oak with intricate carvings of leaves and tiny trees with branches curling up the sides. At each corner were tiny ducks carved in various stages of flight, all pointing outwards from the picture as if leaving the scene with the dogs hot on their feathered tails.

My hands stopped in midair. I could not quite make my fingers touch the beautiful frame. I swallowed hard and took four deep breaths. I clenched my jaws tight and pressed my lips together, fighting the inner conflict of destroying something so beautiful. I dropped my hands back down and shoved them into my pockets, fists clenched tightly, my fingers long past freezing. I stared hard at the picture, willing the delicate etchings on the soft shiny wood to burn to my memory before it burned in the fire.

My head dropped down so my eyes were on the floor as I worked to numb my mind, to make it as numb as my fingers and feet were. My hands would not come out of my pockets. I turned my back to the painting and slowly looked up at the other large painting on the opposite wall.

This was a landscape of shaded green mountains with spruce trees towering above a small shimmering lake where a family of Sitka black-tailed deer grazed among wildflowers. A peaceful scene of quiet serenity - the very essence of this island wilderness. The frame was less decorative—this one was simple, elegant. It set off the placid woodlands to perfection. Again, I paused. This time a sense of lightness came through my body. I took a long, deep breath. The picture seemed to calm my anxiety, relaxing me into a state of inner peace. I felt almost a smile inside, a sprig of courage nudged in my gut.

I gazed at the scene and locked eyes with the doe in the meadow. I saw into those intelligent, gentle eyes and knew things would be okay. As the doe would do everything she could to maintain life, so would I. Sorting through the consequences would come later. I gently lifted the picture off the wall, all the while keeping my eyes on the doe, mesmerized by this peaceful scene and hearing the quiet. It would be okay, I kept telling myself, it would be okay.

I leaned the picture against the wall beside the woodstove facing out so I could look at it for a while longer in its simple frame with its simple grandeur and simple message of peace and survival.

With a tiny spark of hope, I knelt down, picked up the phonebook and began tearing the pages a few at a time, crumpling them into tight wads. Then I carefully opened the door of the stove a few inches to cause a light draft. I could see a tiny glow at the bottom just inside the door. I carefully placed a single wad of phonebook pages close to the glow, another on the other side, and then I tore off another tiny piece and carefully touched the edge of the coal.

It caught, first just a wisp, and then curled upwards. The tiny flame flickered, reached for the wads of paper on the other sides, and ate them. Whoosh! The flames shot up. I jerked my hand back and then quickly tossed in a few more wads. Woof! Again, they caught. I lay a few pieces of the small broken frames over the burning paper and watched as they turned dark brown, then black, burning and catching and lighting with fire and burning. I added a few more small pieces crosswise to those and watched as they too turned brown, then black, then caught up burning, the fire growing higher and higher. I tossed in more wads then more pieces of wooden frames.

I began to feel the heat. The glorious, wonderful, ice-melting, finger-thawing, tear-drying heat. I wanted to crawl into the woodstove. I wanted to feel warm again. I motioned the heat toward my face with both hands and coughed. OK. Too close.

I tossed the last of the smaller wood frame pieces onto the fire and closed the door to encourage the smoke back up the stack and make the fire last longer, burning the wood slowly. I could hang onto the big frames for a while longer, if the fire burned more slowly. Just a little longer.

George raised his head slowly from his crossed arms at the sound of crackling wood. He stepped into the living room, eyes wide, eyebrows raised to his forehead.

"Clare, you got the woodstove going!" George said in obvious bewilderment. "How did you do it? Where'd you get the . . ." His voice drifted down to silence as he saw the frameless photos on the table and the blank spaces on the walls. He jerked his head back to me and caught my red, smoke-filled eyes with his.

I watched the expressions dance across his face in visible stages from bewildered astonishment to incredulity to a satisfaction that was worth every picture frame I burned. His face lit up in amazement then darkened as he recognized the loss, as I had.

George straightened himself up to his full height, inhaled a big breath of air and puffed out with a new resilience and pride at my newly revealed determination. We would not give up. We would keep going. Together we would make it. I could tell by the expression on George's face how much he was overwhelmed at the brilliance of the idea, quickly dismissing the downside, as was his habit when something good could be made out of something not so good. I was beaming and getting warmer.

I was now the determined one. I had picked him up and stood strong when he was floundering. We'd been done for, so he thought. As the inner glow spread up and out, we gazed into each other's eyes, filling each other with a new spark that burned bigger and bigger, George reached for my hands and pulled me up from the floor and into his arms.

He couldn't feel my body as I couldn't feel his through the many layers of clothes—it was like hugging a pile of blankets, but we stood there, locked together in long familiar memories of being just so. There was no sorrow there, no tears, no sadness, no despair. Instead, we each mirrored a calm resilience, a new resourcefulness that reflected a renewed pride and sense of being soul mates, each lifting the other as we danced and sometimes stumbled through life together. George smiled and I smiled back.

"Piece of cake," I said, shrugging nonchalantly with my newfound cocky self-confidence. I had met the challenge, crested the hill, faced the danger, and passed the test, survived by my own wits. I was elated. I had it all figured out now, or so I thought.

We held each other as tight as we could for a long while. Maybe not feeling each other through the many layers, but knowing the feeling well by now. It was wonderful. We listened to the light crackle, pop, pop in the stove, and began to feel some of the warmth. We clung to the moment, not wanting to move, knowing the big frames would need to be broken and burned next, but not yet.

We stayed quiet, tightly holding on, stretching out the moment of hope, clinging to the last lingering moment of bliss. The pops and crackles were getting less frequent and more sporadic, like popcorn when it was almost done. The flame was dying out, the quiet growing louder and becoming a dread. Outside the winds were dying down, too. There was less howling and moaning, less whining and creaking from the bent and whipped-over trees. And something else. Noise. Big noise. Loud, obnoxious thundering, pounding racket.

We both looked up at the same time and caught the glimpse of light that suddenly flashed between the cracks in the curtains. We glanced at each other with raised eyebrows as we pulled back the curtains and peered into the deep dark night.

The snow-covered trees glowed with two yellow circles that bounced unsteadily up and down like two fireflies in sync, from the trees to the road and back up to the trees. It was an eerie spectacle as the dim matching glows bounced along, growing bigger and brighter as they danced their way up the side of the hill.

The thundering boom, boom of an old beaten truck engine protested at the steep climb in banging spurts and sputters, gears grinding and black smoke chugging like a steam locomotive, making frozen dark puffs against the stark white snowbanks. The twin beams turned into our driveway, followed by a huge dump truck with a makeshift snowplow out front, bobbing up and down while making a path to our door.

We were instantly blinded as we stepped out on the deck, like two deer caught in the headlights. Pete opened the truck door and deftly hopped to the ground.

"Figured you guys could use some firewood about now— where ya want it?" hollered Pete over the roaring engine.

He was a tall, wafer-thin man dressed in flannel, fleece, and snow boots that clung to his body in a meager effort to stay on him. He had long straggly brown hair and intelligent, merry brown eyes deep-set into leathery weathered skin. Somewhere underneath the scruffy blond beard and moustache was a thin mouth that carried a booming voice to rival his truck's engine.

"Hey, Pete, man are we glad to see you!" hailed George as he waded through the thigh-high snowdrift, making his way to the truck. "Just over there would be great!" George gestured towards the longish dent in the snow where the woodpile used to be.

We had cut, split, and stacked several cords of wood before the snow came, but halfway through the winter, it was all gone. Apparently, nine dead trees were still not enough. We were ecstatic, tremendously grateful, and completely baffled that Pete had shown up out of the blue . . . or out of the white, in this case.

I grabbed a pitcher of snow and hurried back into the house, scooped it into the empty coffeepot, set it on the pad and lit the burner. When the snow melted, I dumped it in the top, added coffee grounds and set the pot back on the burner. I said a silent "thank you" prayer as hot coffee brewed in the pot.

Pete plowed a notch out of the snowdrift across the driveway and George waved him backwards as the truck slowed to the clearing and dumped a mountain of split wood to the ground. Pete cut the engine and with a few more spurts and sputters, it eventuality died out, leaving a gaping silence in the air.

"Come on in Pete, the coffee's hot," I invited from the patio door.

"Don't mind if I do." Pete handed George a five-gallon container of water from the seat of his truck. Then, balancing two shopping bags, he elbowed the rusty door shut.

Pete owned a sawmill about two miles down the hill from our place. We had stopped there last fall to pick out some lumber to fix the skirting and shim up the blocks on our mobile home. He was a friendly, good-natured guy, long-winded at times with a vast knowledge about the history and people of Kodiak. Pete was born and raised in Kodiak and he had loads of entertaining stories that always began with "Way back when...."

When we pulled into the sawmill lot, we were met by a rowdy pack of five Rottweilers and one Golden Retriever rushing towards us. We stayed in the truck.

"Back," yelled Pete, and the dogs dutifully retreated to the shop. "Security guards," he said, glancing at the pack. "What can I do for ya?" Pete smiled as he opened the truck door. George and Pete shook hands and a long friendship began. He offered valuable tips on the best way to attach wooden planks to the skirting and rig up a deck, and even followed us up the hill that day, his truck piled high with materials.

"Rookies," he roared as he stepped through the trailer door that blustery night. He piled the bags on the counter and cautiously shook snow from his clothes. "I knew you two were rookies from the minute I laid eyes on you. No power out this way when the winds get up," he continued. "You lasted longer than most out here though, I'll say that. Determined or stubborn, I don't know what you are yet, but you ain't doing half bad for your first year up here, perched like birds on the side of this mountain."

He stopped to take a breath and looked around the small kitchen. He frowned when he came to the woodstove with the telltale signs of shredded phonebook and frameless pictures still on the end table. He noted the frost growing on the inside of the windows where the too thin curtains parted with gusts of wind. His head swung back to us and took in the snow hat, mittens, and bathrobe I wore under a parka and then George's fleece-lined jeans and two sweatshirts topped with his parka. With a slight nod and what could have been a small smile of approval, he dragged out a metal kitchen chair and sat down at the table.

"Way back when I was a kid . . ." was how the stories began. We listened intently to long tales full of wit and wistfulness touched with the sadder tones of yesteryear. The stories ended when the coffeepot was empty. I was especially delighted with this friendly historical diversion and felt the strength as well as the warmth come back into my weary spirit.

"Maybe a little of both," he said, as he stood up from his chair, glancing around again and walking to the door. He turned his head back, "Good pie, though." And out he went, back into the dark, cold wintry night.

Pete became a dear friend of ours throughout the years. George would fix some electrical anomaly at Pete's place, Pete would come by unexpectedly, bringing wood or plowing away the huge snowdrifts that buried the trailer and driveway and road in one smooth blanket of white snow. He told us more tales, I poured more coffee and George asked more questions about

Kodiak. Sometimes we sat at the tiny table and exchanged a few how- to's on surviving the elements, and griped about paying the "exorbitant" costs of living on Kodiak.

Pete seemed to sense how close we had come to giving up that winter. His stories were inspirational, motivating, challenging us not to give up. It was a hard life up there, not like the cushiony one we had left behind, where lights were always on, city snowplows and trash collectors ran regular schedules, and winter was only a few weeks of ankle-deep snow and darkness turned back to daylight in no time.

That winter was the first sign of discontent I had seen in George. He thought we had made a mistake and I knew what would come next. We had sat for a long time in that icy trailer, listening to the winds scream and howl against the frosted windows, drowning out the sounds of normal conversation.

It was one of the worst snowstorms in Kodiak history that winter. The blizzard slammed into the trailer, rocking it back and forth. One time, before the snow completely buried it, we took the dog and sat in the truck, turning the heater on for short periods. We were shivering, cold, and thoroughly discouraged that first winter way up on that mountain, not sure what to do next. Pete had saved us, in more ways than one.

George and I started early the following year. Not wanting to run out of wood again, we dragged no less than twelve trees from the ravine that had fallen over during the many windstorms of past years. We were going to be on top of it next year.

Digging Out

11 LAST HAUL

It was late October and we were loading the last pile of cut logs into the large bucket attached to the ATV four-wheeler. When the bucket was full it had to be towed to the top of our lot and around to the chopping area. The lower side of our property sloped down to the ravine, making a slight grade on the path leading up to the trailer.

George heaved the last round into the bucket and nodded for me to get on the bike and drive it up the hill. A patch of ice had formed the night before just before the crest at the top so I had to gun the throttle to get up enough speed to make it up. A few feet from the top, I felt the tires sliding on the ice. All four tires had a set of chains wrapped around them for traction in snow, but they started slipping and spinning on the ice.

The full load was heavy and the bike started sliding back down the hill. In a panic to stop the backward roll, I put my foot down just as my mind registered the warning George had given me several times before. "Whatever happens, don't put your feet down." Too late.

My ankle-length boot slid back on the ice and I lost my balance. The bike tipped precariously sideways to the left. I grabbed the right handlebar, which happened to be the accelerator, desperately trying to hold on. The heavy chained tires whined and screamed beneath me as I struggled to stay on the ATV.

A sudden tug on my left leg jerked me down and backwards. My head was now level with the gas tank, my right leg draped awkwardly across the top of the seat and my right arm stretched out, still clinging to the accelerator handle grip. My boot string caught around the back axle as it spun wildly around and around, pulling my foot under the chained tire, grinding my leg into the ice.

As boot followed string, up and around the rusty metal axle between the tires, I finally let go of the accelerator and dropped sideways off the bike with a heavy thump. I hit the ice hard, taking most of the brunt on my left shoulder and hip. The tires mercifully stopped spinning.

George charged up the hill, slipping and sliding, desperate to reach me and halt the machine. He quickly switched off the angry thing and pulled it off my leg, untangling the boot string with a swift slice of his knife. I glimpsed a flash of horror on his face as he scanned me over from head to mangled boot and shredded, blood-spattered pant leg.

George didn't say a word as he untangled my boot from the axle and carefully moved my leg away from the monster tires. He carried me over to a tree stump, brushed the rocks, mud, and dirty ice from my face, and then turned away. He started the bike, drove it on up the hill and around to the unloading area.

My leg burned like fire but I didn't want to look at it. I needed to think of something else. Anything to keep back the tears and shock and to stay in control. I hummed a few bars of an old song as loud as I could, and concentrated on an eagle perched in the tree above, his smooth white feathered-head with its black beady eyes glaring down at me, and the trees, and their long green branches sticking straight out covered in fuzzy green moss like so many sweater sleeves, and gray rough bark slipping up underneath like umbrella poles - any diversion would do. I continued to force a swirl of thoughts rapidly through my brain, keeping the pain at bay for as long as possible. I had learned how to do that well years ago.

After several minutes, I took a few deep breaths and forced my trembling body to quiet. When I felt back in control, I surveyed the damage. The pant leg of my fleece-lined jeans was shredded up to the knee but the thick material seemed to have shielded most of my leg. There were two deep gashes and several angry red marks on the calf in the distinct pattern of tire chain links, and I knew my ankle was twisted.

Well, maybe I didn't have it all figured out yet, not perfectly. I still needed lots of advice and some heavy oversight at times, but I gathered up my best upbeat and positive attitude, and limped on. I wore those chain-link scars for several years after that, and wouldn't get on a four-wheeler for even longer.

George was never much on sympathy, but he made up for it in love. Too much sympathy in the moment makes a person weak in the face of disaster, where a firm reality check and a "Next time…" comment quickly diverts the self-pity and puts things back into perspective.

Over the next four years, we rose to the challenge of those harsh winters on the hill, and tried out several ideas to keep our trailer cozy and warm. We used plywood for skirting, and then lined it with bats of insulation duct-taped to the inside (which lasted only a year once the moisture pulled the soggy mess to the ground). We tacked up space blankets stuffed with a year's worth of newspapers and old blankets and tattered sleeping bags bought from the Salvation Army but that didn't keep out the worst cold.

We finally acquired eight panels, 12 feet long by 4 feet wide and 8 inches thick, which had been used in refrigerator trucks discarded at the dump. Each panel consisted of dense Styrofoam sandwiched between 2-inch aluminum sheets. We carefully trimmed each section to size and fixed them to the insides of the skirting. Next, we covered the ground under the trailer with black plastic sheeting, and then layered old cardboard boxes flattened out and duct-taped together, making one long brown cardboard floor. For looks, it wouldn't make it in *Better Homes and Gardens*, but the pipes didn't freeze as much.

I changed out the pillowcase curtains for folded and hemmed fleece blankets and sealed the windows with cut-to-size pieces of wool blanket secured in place with tacks and duct tape. With well-stocked shelves of basic essentials: batteries, matches, propane, water, coffee, sugar, and powdered cream stashed in airtight containers along with several cases of food and a corner of newspapers stacked floor to ceiling in the spare bedroom, we were in. Gradually, we were figuring out this survival thing. We were back to our upbeat and positive selves and feeling confident. Complacent, even.

12 OPPORTUNISTS

The long-awaited fishing season came once again, and the rains had finally stopped for the moment. The temperature climbed to forty-eight degrees on one lovely June morning, the sunshine warm and welcome. George and I headed out for a drive to the end of the forty-mile road. Along the way, we spotted eagles, ravens, and a rabbit as it leapt out of sight, its fluffy fur coat now ashy brown except for a white puffy tail and large white feet.

The thick fur of the snowshoe hare had been completely white last winter then gradually changed to brown as daylight increased. This seasonal cloak of disguise kept the rabbits well hidden from predators like fox, eagles, and bears. They were tasty, if a bit chewy, and many hunters along with their braying beagles traipsed after them through the open fields, hoping to catch an easy meal. We heard a few shots in the distance from a .22 rifle and I said a silent prayer for the rabbits.

We motored slowly along the dusty dirt road and generally enjoyed the beautiful view of snowcapped mountains rising from emerald green fields of grasses and shrubs that stretched up and over Kalsin Bay hill on the right. The deep blue bay waters

on the left lay flat under the calm wind. It was a perfect day for
a drive or to be out in a boat.

A few miles later George stopped the truck and we got out
and walked to the shore. We stood on Roselyn Beach clasping
hands and watching two boats drifting along the bay, probably
fishing for cod or halibut. Seagulls circled above the boats at
close range, just in case the fishermen lost a fish or dropped
some bait in the water.

An opportunist, that's what seagulls were, I thought. They
waited and watched for the next chance of someone leaving
something tasty behind. Some called them scavengers, I suppose.
I thought they seemed a lot like some people I knew—waiting
and watching for the next opportunity to get a promotion, or
for that special outfit to go on sale, or perhaps most admirably,
waiting for the next best friend to come along.

George, for instance, was one such opportunist. He offered a
friendly handshake, a nod of his ball-capped head and a friendly
greeting to any stranger. I, on the other hand shied away from
meeting people, afraid of appearing awkward or saying the
wrong thing. What I lacked in social skills, George easily made
up for.

He possessed an air of self-confidence and an easy manner
that naturally drew people to him, which meant an abundance of
friends and acquaintances frequently appeared at our door. He
listened to them complain about where they came from, and then
shared his tales of adventures and life on the Emerald Island.

He speckled conversations with stories of humor, danger,
and of course, his favorite topic, the all-time biggest fish he'd
caught lately. People naturally warmed to his friendly and generous personality. He started every friendship with an eagerness to
show them the beauty and bounty of Kodiak.

He readily offered fishing tips, along with the best places
to catch whatever fish they happened to be targeting. George
took his new friends on their first fishing trip in his well-used
and weathered aluminum skiff. It was no easy feat, taking out

greenhorns. Some people got seasick, couldn't hold their footing, or weren't physically fit to pull up a heavy water-soaked gill net or decent-sized fish.

After living here for several years, George and I had learned, sometimes the hard way that fishing in Kodiak waters was not like other places. It took strength, determination, a certain amount of skill and as George would say, "upbeat and positive thinking." But the rewards were well worth it. The fish were huge, good eating, and by far the cleanest, brightest, prettiest fish we had ever caught. In our later years, we often reminisced about the thrill of the first fish hooked, as well as the first boat, the first soaker, the first bite, the first strain of muscles against that huge fish ranging in size from a small child to a full sheet of plywood.

George introduced himself to Walter, who had arrived in the spring from Mississippi, and had never caught a fish bigger than eight inches. George began that friendship like many others - by offering to take Walter fishing, Kodiak-style.

"Got some boots? Get a good rod and a fishing license and let's go." It was Walter's first fishing trip on the ocean. It was early morning, partly cloudy, with three-foot waves rolling easy on a slack tide. They cast off in the seventeen-foot metal skiff, George in the back straddling the throttle of the forty-horse motor, cruising past the cannery docks at slow speed. Walter sat in the bow, wide-eyed and smiling as he took in the beauty of the smooth blue water, green-treed hillsides, and multicolored houses as they slowly slid by.

George kept the pace slow and easy for Walter. The engine puttered the skiff out to Buoy 4, slicing through waves and leaving a V-shaped trail of white foamy water. George slowed the motor, then cut the engine and waited for a count of three while the boat drifted over to his favorite spot.

"Drop the anchor, Walter." George stood up to catch the wind direction as the boat settled against the anchor line. With the swiftness of a seasoned angler, George grabbed his rod, baited the hook and dropped the line down to the bottom.

"Will do." Walter hung onto the side of the boat with one hand and heaved the anchor over the side with the other. He stood up to reach for his rod, then sat back down with a hard thump. He couldn't quite get his feet situated to the rhythm of the rocking boat.

George stepped over, reached the rod, baited the hook, and held it out to Walter. He showed him how to drop the line without creating a "bird's nest" by gently placing a thumb on the line as it peeled off the reel. When the one-pound weight hit the bottom of the ocean, the line went slack. He reeled about two inches back up. "That way you know your bait is close to the bottom," George explained. "'Cause that's where the fish are."

In a matter of minutes, Walter's rod tugged down, tugged again, and then pulled hard, bending the rod tip down to the water.

"George!" He shouted, "I think the line is caught on something down there. Probably a truck or a car or whatever you have in this ocean!" His arms stretched stiff as he gripped the rod handle with both hands. His head jerked back again at George.

"Nope, you got a halibut, Walter," George shouted back with eager anticipation.

"A what?"

"A halibut. Now reel down and then pull the rod up. Reel, reel, reel quick. Keep the rod tip up, reel, reel, reel, down, down, down, pull the rod tip up, reel faster, down, down, reel up, up, up, don't horse it, now keep it up, down, down, down, reel, reel, reel," George stood next to Walter mimicking Walter's body as he continued his bizarre instructions in Walter's ear.

Walter, bent at the waist, his back hunched over the rod handle, gripped the rod between aching white knuckles as he reeled in the line. He leaned backwards, pulling hard as his muscles strained against the weight of the huge fish. The fish tugged him over again as Walter reeled himself into a frenzy. He held on to the rod with a death grip and tugged back again as hard as he could. He had no idea what this was all about, but with George yelling in his ear, he could only do as he was told.

The boat rocked back and forth, as he held on to the rod and turned the crank on the reel with superglued fingertips. The end of the rod handle was jabbed deep into his gut as Walter tried to keep the rod tip up and reel down.

"This is like pulling on a truck that won't budge," cried Walter. "Are you sure this is a fish?" He pulled, reeled and held tight. Then the rod jerked hard and the line on the reel began peeling off fast. The fish was running; the battle was on.

"When a halibut runs, you just gotta hang on," George shouted. "Don't worry about cranking the reel, just hold on." The monster fish suddenly stopped with only a few inches remaining on the reel.

"Reel , reel, reel, down, down, down, reel, reel, reel," George ranted again. He knew the fish was just gathering strength for another run. "Fast as you can reel, man, reel!" It was another forty minutes before an exhausted Walter dragged the halibut close to the surface.

"It's as big as a house!" Walter stammered. It was indeed a large flatfish, brown skin speckled with black dots on one side and creamy white on the other. The two fish eyes on the same side of its head stared up at Walter and George. It took another twenty minutes to position the fish close enough to the boat.

"Bring it closer to the side, Walter. Keep it under the water; now drag it over, a little closer." George stood with the gaff poised and ready in his hand and shaking with excitement.

The sleeping giant suddenly breached the surface, its eyes glaring at its captors in the sun. It was getting ready to run for it again.

"Grab the gun, grab the gun!" George dropped the gaff, grabbed the rod and shouted at Walter while grappling with the frantic, fighting monster.

"What?" Walter stumbled around in confusion, not sure he heard right.

"Grab the gun and shoot it!"

"What are you talking about, shoot it? We don't shoot fish where I come from!"

"Shoot the fish, just shoot it, Walter! Never mind, get the gaff."

After strenuous effort, excitement, and argument, they finally hauled the 165-pound giant up and over the side of the boat. It slapped down hard on the deck with a solid thud. But they weren't done yet.

"Walter, drop the rod, grab that rope, and get on top of this thing before it gets its second wind," barked George, holding down the fish with both hands.

"What? Sit on the fish; sit on top of the fish?" Walter stammered around on one foot then the other hesitating near the fish in awkward confusion. Of course, it was a second too late. The fish came back to life and flapped up and down like a bucking bronco. The tail smacked down hard against the bottom of the boat repeatedly in fast furious motion beating on the deck with the force of a giant sledgehammer. Its mouth gaped open showing enormous razor teeth and the gills flapped up and down in its struggle to get free. The boat rocked back and forth, leaning dangerously close to the water. The deck became slippery and slimy with blood and seawater.

Walter grabbed the tail while George pounced on top of the fish and wrapped the rope around the huge head and inside the gills, barely missing the jagged teeth snapping at the air. He slipped the rope down and around its tail and pulled it tight into a knot. When they finished, the fish lay hogtied, tail to head, as it slowly gave up the struggle and settled down on the deck.

Walter sat back and jerked off his hat, wiping the sweat, slime, and grime from his face. "Whew! That is the biggest fish I've ever seen in my life, George, let alone caught! It was like catching a truck!" His eyes were wide as saucers as he stared at the prize halibut finally dead on the deck. George sliced the neck to bleed out the gills, and then sat back next to Walter to admire the monster fish. It was a keeper, for sure.

There were many such trips that George and Walter shared together, many such opportunities that brought them together. Their friendship grew strong and continued through the years even after Walter eventually departed from the Emerald Isle.

13 ON BUILDING A HOUSE

Building a house was a lot like building a relationship–it required a good foundation to start with. It was a slow and sometimes painful process, often fraught with problems and mistakes. Things went wrong and sometimes considerable changes had to be made along the way.

In the beginning there was all the excitement and anticipation of something happening that would be lasting and beautiful. Board by board, nail by nail the work began. Understanding and commitment formed the walls of protection against the outside world. Compliments had to be liberally applied and soft words of adoration spread throughout, like glossy paint and carpet.

This building process was slow and frustrating and mistakes were inevitable. Some houses lasted for centuries, and some deteriorated quickly due to lack of diligent maintenance and care. A house had to be nurtured with subtle changes made occasionally to avoid boredom within its walls. Above all, care had to be taken to ensure it was a place of peace and tranquility, refuge and relaxation at the end of a long day.

It was a wet, rainy May of 1998. Kodiak was teeming with activity, despite the drizzly, miserable weather we'd been having for the last three weeks. The annual Crab Festival, scheduled consistently during Memorial Day weekend for more than fifty years, was in full swing.

The hearty people came to have fun, dressed in yellow slickers, droplets making trails down arms and backs, hoods pulled over their heads to keep out the drizzle, eager tucked-in faces lined up for Bruin burgers, meat on a stick, and of course, the famous crab cakes, along with the usual cotton candy and ice cream.

Children's rides were set up and operated by volunteers, including a ferris wheel, a tilt-a-whirl, and slow-moving miniature airplanes that swung happy, laughing kids around in a circle. Various booths sold trinkets and T-shirts and hand-crafted items, from salmon skin belts to wooden carvings of eagles, bears, and fishing boats expertly sculpted with a chainsaw from spruce tree stumps. There were informational booths handing out pamphlets advertising the local phone company or military recruiting or health services offered at the small local hospital. It was a celebration of the bounty of the sea and triggered the beginning of the fishing season.

On Memorial Day at the appointed hour, local fishing families gathered for the moving Fisherman's Memorial Service to honor those lost at sea during the past year. There followed the traditional ringing of the bell as each name was solemnly pronounced and then a few moments of silence in remembrance of loved ones.

Commercial fishing vessels were blessed as they slipped out of the harbor, with captains and crews eager to begin long days and nights of vigorous, backbreaking, but rewarding work. Most would return to off-load thousands of pounds of fish from their lucrative hauls and celebrate boisterously at the local bars.

By this time, three restaurants had closed and two new ones opened, and Wal-Mart announced the opening of a small-scale store. Kodiak was becoming "civilized."

"Let's build a house, Clare," said George, excitement shining in his crystal blue eyes that so often reminded me of the ocean waters on a calm sunny day. After four long years of fixing frozen pipes, covering drafty windows and shoveling snow from the roof of the trailer, it was indeed time we built a house.

Construction on our new house, like our relationship, began tentatively. We were both unsure and inexperienced, but confident that all would work out well. We had a solid foundation but at times, the struggles were enormous, seemingly insurmountable, and problems occurred that we were not prepared for. Nevertheless, at the end of this building process came safety, security, and protection—like two birds in a cozy nest, we survived, and the house was beautiful, when finally completed.

We had located a contractor (one of only three on the island at the time), plans were developed and the paperwork signed. In October 1998 the project began. We had no idea what we were getting into. Some lessons we learned the hard way, with drastic consequences that seriously challenged our self-proclaimed motto of being upbeat and positive.

Rule number one: Nobody worked as fast as we could, in our minds! Our premise that we could have poured concrete, pounded nails, and painted walls so much faster ourselves, left us pulling our hair out, pounding on floorboards, and putting up such a fuss that later (much later) I almost felt sorry for that contractor.

He was an expert craftsman, to be sure, but fairly new to the area, which meant he was not aware of the four-to six-week wait for supplies and materials to arrive by barge from Seattle. The lag time (or was it slacking-off time) between shipments was long and annoying, and made even more so by wrong colors or dimensions of products, which then had to be returned and reshipped in the correct specifications.

The word "whatever" often passed my lips during those times, followed by a deep sigh and rolling of my eyes. George, too, became gloomy and downcast as time seemed to be wasting and winter pressed closer and the process dragged on. And on.

The cement truck finally arrived in early November and the men worked well into the night scraping and smoothing out the runny piles of gray gritty goop. Gigantic Herman Nelson propane-powered machines were hooked up to temporary power and blew great gusts of heated air to maintain the required 40-degree temperature for curing the cement for the 1200 square feet of garage floor and four feet of pony wall that created the perimeter of the house. Three weeks later, it was determined to be "set" and it was another two weeks before the first shipment of lumber arrived and workers showed up again.

"It will go up quick, you'll see," George said, trying to appease my anxious look at the sky as snowflakes drifted down to the empty ground. This was a phrase George was to utter many times, much to my consternation, and on rare occasions, I managed to catch brief flashes of doubt and frustration even on the face of Mr. Optimistic himself.

The huge trucks hauling shipping containers of precious building materials arrived at last. We pulled up to our driveway, but had to stop and park on the side of the road. Two trucks filled the entire driveway plus half the yard. But they were here! We rushed towards the trucks, and then stopped, deciding not to interrupt.

The workers were actually working. The men unloaded each piece like ants moving purposefully from truck to yard, yard to truck, the stack of lumber growing wider and taller as the daylight grew dimmer.

We walked over, grabbed a board, George on one end and me on the other, and pitched in. We didn't want them to leave before the trucks were empty. Maybe if we helped, it would not only go faster, it might entice them to finish the job. Or not. They stopped at their usual five o'clock, got in their trucks, and drove away.

It was after nine that night when George and I off-loaded the last board, covered everything with blue tarps, pulling them around and under the end boards with a fistful of bungee cords, and crawled into our truck. We turned on the heater full blast and sat there.

In silent companionship, we eased each other's anger and frustration, and enjoyed the welcome sense of accomplishment. It was done. We leaned into each other for a quick kiss, and then George got out, walked over to the temporary power switch to turn off the spotlight, got back in the truck and drove us to the trailer.

The framing seemed to move along at a steady pace as the shape of our 40-foot-wide by 90-foot-long ranch-style structure began to take shape. We designed our own house plans, and not surprisingly, it turned out like an overgrown trailer. Apparently, we hadn't ventured too far from our "roots." In actuality, it matched the landscape, matched the direction of the rising and setting of the sun, placed the garage at an easy distance from the road for ease of moving the boat in and out, and most important, it included the well.

That is to say, the well was now *inside* the garage, located about two feet from the far wall. The exposed earth containing the six-inch metal wellcasing pipe was encircled by a two-foot square of wooden blocks about twelve inches high. The water pipe connected to the bladder tank, connected to the wellhead, moved up the far wall of the garage, across the ceiling and into the house, with the expectation that the water pipes would never freeze again.

The house footprint and design of interior spaces were strategically planned to gain the most from the sun's warmth, the ocean view, and practical advantage of location against hurricane-force winds and frigid temperatures. This is not to say it was perfect.

The garage measured 40 feet by 35 feet, to accommodate not only two vehicles, but also two four-wheelers, a 20-foot boat and a heavy-duty Bobcat. A woodstove stood in the far corner,

George's workbench in the other, with various tools, racks, and brooms hanging on walls lined with shelves for pieces and parts.

The living quarters measured 40 by 55 feet and included a combined kitchen and dining room, a living room, three bedrooms and two bathrooms. I chose light maple cabinets, white tile sporting tiny wine-red flowers with green leaves and spruce green carpeting that enhanced my sense of the trees and grass and wildflowers waiting outside my windows. It was easy to think of the result rather than the process.

The "pearl gray" toilets were returned posthaste along with the matching sinks in exchange for white, and the astonishingly colored flooring for both bathrooms was quickly rejected and replaced with more flooring that was suitable. I had neglected to plan for a linen closet but the hot water tank fed my shower first, saving precious water wasting away until it turned warm enough to climb in. George was not as sensitive, thankfully.

The war with each other that everyone who had built a house warned us about didn't happen. We simply divided it up. George decided all things for the garage; I decided all things for the living area. Piece of cake. It was the other war that had made us nuts.

By mid December, the house was "dried in," including exterior walls, windows, doors, and a shiny new green metal roof (quickly exchanged from an ugly blue). The plumbing work was running smoothly, accomplished by a great and generous certified plumber who was also a longtime friend, and the electricity was being managed by a lead electrician, a helper, George, and me (I fancied myself a general laborer).

Miles of wire snaked between studs connecting to blue plastic boxes used to contain outlets and light switches. It all circled around to the breaker boxes connecting through the 200-amp panel and curled into the box up to the breakers. The maze of copper pipes stretched under the crawlspace connecting to the hot water tank, bathrooms, laundry room, and finally up to the kitchen sink and dishwasher.

Two men on stilts laid insulation and sheetrock on top of the studs. They expertly lifted and fixed the heavy panels in place, balancing on wooden poles like two circus clowns. They matched each other stride for stride from one end of the garage to the other end of the house. It was an art, a skill that was both amazing and entertaining to watch.

We seemed to be back on track. Everything was moving along like clockwork. It was the middle of December and I was even thinking we might be snug in our new house by Christmas. I foolishly began dreaming about where the Christmas tree would go, how the lights would look, and what decorations to put up. I pictured my new dining room table sitting in the center of the kitchen, aglow with candles and a nativity set, and a pretty red table cloth. I would hang frosty green wreathes from each window and curl tinsel around the doorframes. And then the bubble busted.

The contractor sauntered into the garage, dressed in clean jeans, clean shirt and sparkling white tennis shoes. No tool belt dangled from his waist and no work gloves covered his hands. Not good. He cheerily announced he was leaving the island for a vacation. My thoughts were that he and his family would be visiting relatives on the mainland for Christmas and I heartily wished him well. We would see him right after Christmas. No, said he, it would actually be about the middle of January when he returned.

"The interior of the house is all ready to paint. Will you be doing that before you leave?" George asked. The contractor shook his head, smiling.

"Nope. We'll paint when I get back."

"But we can't finish the electrical and plumbing until after the walls are painted. We have workers standing by right now to finish tying in the utilities but they can't do that until the painting is done," reasoned George.

"Well, that can come later," was the contractor's almost jo-vial response, obviously happy to be on his way.

"But that's a whole month from now. Are you gonna just leave this project unfinished for a whole month?" George kept his tone calm but the incredulity was barely concealed.

"We'll get on it as soon as I get back. I just came by to let you know I'm leaving." He walked back to his truck, opened the door, waved, and called back, "Merry Christmas!" as he sped out of the driveway.

After two days of sulking, George woke me up on the morning of Christmas Eve.

"I got a plan," George said, shaking my shoulder.

"Great, George," I mumbled, blinking the sleep from my eyes. I was lately wary about George's plans. I had unreasonably concluded that his plans were what got us into this nightmare in the first place.

"We'll paint the house ourselves." George's eyes were bright with enthusiasm as he playfully began dragging me from my nice cozy bed.

"George. George. Stop and wait a minute. It's Christmas Eve. Where are you going to get paint and brushes and all that stuff?" I was hoping this detail would squelch the plan, but true to George, he was up early, had already made a few phone calls and established that the hardware store and rental shop were both open until noon. Spiffy.

It took us two and a half days of backbreaking, muscle-searing work to prime, paint, and double paint 3,600 square feet of walls and ceilings from one end of the house to the other end of the garage. George operated the sprayer while I hauled the empty paint containers and brought back full ones. I followed him from wall to wall with a small paintbrush to smooth out any drips and point out any areas needing touch-ups. Overall, it didn't turn out too bad, for a couple of amateurs.

After we peeled off white-speckled raingear, gloves, masks, and shower caps, we plopped down on overturned milk crates in silence. It was midnight on the second day after Christmas. We could see tiny white flakes of snow through the window in the kitchen, silently making their way to the ground to mix with the already six inches of accumulation.

George raised his hand with visible effort, as did I. His can of Coors Light inched towards mine, we clinked them together, raised them upwards, and then took long, refreshing sips.

"Done," we said at the same time, and clanked our cans down on the bare wooden floorboards. Another milestone accomplished. I began reciting the poem again that we had concocted while in our working mode, a diversion that provided much comic relief from the tedious chore, and seemed like a creative means to vent our frustrations:

On Building a House

'Twas the night before Christmas at this unfinished house
Not a worker was stirring, not even a mouse

The sheetrock was hung on the walls with such care
But where were the painters, the trim work, the stairs?

The roof was on tight and the siding complete
But inside was freezing, no water, no heat

When out on the driveway there rose such a clatter
The workers were leaving, no bother, no matter

As they drove out of sight, we could hear them all sing
"Have a nice winter, we'll see ya next spring."

We stood on bare floorboards with one candle lit
My wondering eyes filled with tears when they quit

No Christmas tree stood, no tinsel, no present
No turkey was cooked, no smells that were pleasant

George blew out the candle and took off his cap
We then settled down for a cold winter's nap.

By the time the contractors returned, the house was ready for the installation of cabinets, appliances, and flooring. We compromised yet again on the island in the kitchen, but other than that, the project progressed without further mishap. The housing inspector came, signed off and went, and we carefully negotiated a final payment with the contractor, deducting the cost of paint and sprayer rental fees (which caused a minor ruckus, but we would not relent) and compiled a list of small items yet to be completed.

The contractor agreed with all, took the check, and said he would be back. After four months of requesting and pestering and demanding and waiting, we got the hint and finally fixed most of the items ourselves. Eventually, the remaining items became unimportant in the scheme of things.

On 2 February 1999, Groundhog Day, we moved into to our nice new house. Never again did we shout, scream, or curse at frozen pipes. Power outages were still frequent but a backup generator kept the important appliances going, and the structure stood strong and waterproof during the winter storms, sideways rain and hurricane-force winds.

Our house was not perfect; it had its tiny flaws and required constant maintenance and nurturing as the years went by, but it was beautiful and kept us safe and protected against the outside world, becoming the peaceful retreat we had hoped. As we celebrated our 25th anniversary the following month, we were happy and content with our relationship, as well.

14 THE YEAR OF THE BEAR

The snow had finally melted down to the last two-inch clump that used to be a seven-foot snow bank. It was the middle of May, well into spring in other places, but it was late coming to Kodiak this year. The first run of salmon was late coming to the rivers, as well.

The bears were already awake from their long winter's nap, dangerously hungry and restless in search of food. The smell of trash in the dumpsters was too hard to resist. The bears plodded down the roads away from the empty rivers and into the residential neighborhoods. They went stealthily at first, becoming bolder as the long days of no fish urged them towards the easy pickings.

It was early in the morning. The skies were overcast and drizzling in a gray shadowy mist that swirled slowly around the trees and alder bushes, wisping across the yard like veils of gauze in the cool breeze. I stepped out of the door behind the dog, my head tucked under my hood, balancing a coffee cup in one hand and holding my coat closed with the other. My eyes followed Nightmare as he eagerly trotted out a few feet ahead. He was our second Lab, five years old and in his prime. His shiny black fur lay smooth and thick on his back, his satiny ears flapped lightly in the breeze and his tail swayed at the mist. He stopped suddenly in midstride.

He lifted his head and sniffed the air in large quick whiffs. I stopped short just behind him. Thick brushy hackles stood stiff on his back in a long, spiky ridge. A low growl gargled in his throat as he fixed on the object. A sudden chill slipped down my back and my own neck hairs rose. I raised my eyes and looked over the dog's head, past his nose, in a straight line out towards the driveway, and there he was.

The biggest bear I had ever seen stood on all fours about thirty feet in front of us. The gauzy mist swirled around him, snaking under his large girth and between his tree-trunk legs. The huge dark chocolate bear saw us at the same moment and stopped still. Shock and terror made me immobile. I tried frantically to think what to do. In four giant leaps I could be back inside the house, but what about the dog? I whispered his name as I tried frantically to work out a plan. "Nightmare, Nightmare." The dog kept his stance and stared hard at the bear. His legs were rigid, locked in a determined showdown. His lips curled up slightly, showing white gleaming teeth in a silent snarl.

The bear stood where he was, just as determined. I could see his nostrils widen as he took in our scent. His massive head leaned out slightly; a light-colored patch of fur marked his forehead like a menacing helmet. The large hump on his back twitched, sending ripples down his thick brown fur. His claws reached out a good four inches from his pan-sized paws before curving down to tapered points that jabbed into the packed dirt driveway.

Amazing what ran through your mind in a moment of terror: What was that bear doing in our driveway? Had we left any trash outside? Did he think I was a rabbit? Would he fit through this door?

At that instant, I felt the burn on my hand from drops of spilled coffee when I had stopped abruptly. "Ouch," I complained aloud, and then realized the spell was broken. Now or never. I threw the coffee cup at the bear, grabbed Nightmare's collar, ran to the door, opened it and shoved the dog and myself inside and slammed it shut. I foolishly braced against it for the inevitable charge from the bear. Nothing.

After a couple of deep breaths and several long, terrorized seconds, I dared a peek out the window. The bear was licking the inside of the coffee cup on the ground in front of him and alternately licking the damp patches of fur the coffee had made on his left paw.

Still a bit shaky but relieved we got away, I slowly grinned to a chuckle at the comical scene of the big burly bear slurping the last drop of coffee and cleaning his coffee-stained paws. It put a smile on my face for months to come - at those odd times when a sudden flash of memory flicked through my mind. I was positive he didn't feel the burn as I did on my hand.

We watched several bears wander through our yard that year, as did several other residents that lived closer to town. Unfortunately, as they became more and more of a threat to people, a record eight bears were killed that year, one of them while he tried to get through a doggy door, after smelling the dog food just inside. He became stuck up to his shoulders after gnawing the wood around the edges of the small door. The occupant shot him from an upstairs window.

We watched a bear crawl out of a dumpster late one evening a few days later. George lifted the heavy lid with one hand and swung the bag toward the opening, then quickly changed his mind. He dropped the lid, ran back to the truck and jumped in, still clutching the trash bag. "Bear," was all he said in a nervous, excited whisper.

We sat silent and waited. After a few moments, we saw the huge bear lift the lid cautiously, push it back on its hinges and slowly crawl out, one paw at a time, pulling himself up onto the narrow rim of the metal "bear-proof" container, then plop down to the ground in one graceful fluid motion. He lifted a few sacks out, then trotted back into the woods, the white plastic bags clutched in his jaws like a mother carrying her young.

Another day found a young bear napping at the end of our neighbor's driveway, belly to the ground, hind legs sprawled out, front paws crossed over pillowing his massive head. After several loud honks from the car horn, it slowly got up and plodded down the road and back into the woods.

During that fluke of Mother Nature that left the bears so desperate for food, not one person or pet was threatened or injured. The bears were hungry and with no fish in the rivers, resorted to the easiest means to get a meal. The result of so many dead bears dampened our spirits and made us painfully aware of the impact the loss of salmon would have on this community, where man and animals make every effort to coexist and share this gift from the sea.

Bear Warning

15 VISITORS

A happy day it was when friends arrived for a visit and a happy day it was when they departed. Although we missed them when they were gone and laughed at the events and adventures we shared with them, George and I breathed a sigh of relief with each goodbye, as peace of mind and quiet returned to our hilltop home.

Our biggest concern was safety. Visitors came unprepared for the wildness of this remote island. Most people lacked the level of physical fitness required to haul in the one hundred-plus pounds of fish tugging on the end of a rod or climb up and down thin ladders or diving platforms to get in and out of a boat.

They didn't heed even the strictest warnings about wandering alone in the forest or wearing the proper clothing and carrying the necessary survival gear. They didn't seem to realize that once out to sea or into the woods, there was no protection from the many disastrous incidents that could occur.

George and I watched over them like mother hens, and learned to ease them into our rigorous lifestyle. Some caught on to our strange activities and eagerly participated in such tedious tasks as scooping out bloody fish innards, tearing off yellow poisonous lungs from finger-piercing crabs, and waking up every two hours to check the doneness of smoking salmon. Others scowled at this "uncivilized" way of life and departed on the next plane. Still, visitors brought much laughter and fun and great companionship, however brief, to our daily lives.

After the house was built, they came in droves. Each year we hosted four or five sets of visitors that took up entire summers, but it was a joy to show them our beloved island and get them involved in our unique way of life, ready or not.

We had built a small structure behind the house as an add-on to the trailer, which we quickly turned into a guesthouse. It became the destination of choice for repeated visits of friends and relatives.

Visitors came from all over the lower 48. To them, it was a trip of a lifetime, the Alaskan adventure, complete with extreme fishing, sightseeing, and bear viewing. It was a unique experience, not for the faint of heart or light of pocketbook. For us, it was a chance to show off the best place in the world. We enjoyed their company and although it took time and no small effort to be the best hosts we could be, it was truly a labor of love.

It was 10:30 p.m. in mid June. The alders, spruce trees, and wildflowers were in full bloom and bursting with energy. The legendary midnight sun was at its peak, showing off the long-awaited twenty hours of daylight. The sun was still high in the sky as we drove through the still lively town on our way to the airport.

We watched the 11:00 p.m. flight on the Dash 8 aircraft drop from the sky, glide low over the ocean, and land gracefully on the runway. We spotted Patrick and Jake through the large glass window as they arrived from Dallas, and we grinned at the now-familiar scenario as they walked in and glanced around the small, one-room airport.

"Wow, is this really the airport? We thought they were just dropping us off to catch a commuter train or bus or something to the main terminal."

"Nope," George said, shaking hands with the young men, both clean-cut, in their mid thirties, and visibly travel-weary. "This is all there is."

"Welcome to Kodiak, you guys." I stepped forward, shaking hands in turn with our friends, introduced a few years ago by mutual acquaintances during a trip we had made to Texas. We gathered the multitude of luggage and headed for the door. They followed with raised eyebrows, heads swinging from side to side, taking it all in.

It was the beginning of a long commentary of Wows, Oh Wows, and Oh My Gods. Kodiak had that effect on most new arrivals. As we stepped outside, the sun hit the newbies and we grinned again at the anticipated comments.

"I thought we were getting here late. What time is it?"

"Oh, about eleven", answered George with a grin.

"At night?"

"Yep, at night." George lifted the hatch on his 1999 Dodge Ram truck. He put the bags into the back, followed by backpacks and more luggage as Patrick and Jake pivoted their heads around at the mountains, green trees, and bushes and gradually found the last patches of snow up on the tallest peaks.

"Wow, this place is beautiful, George! Google Earth doesn't do it justice!" Jake said, his face radiating excitement and open enthusiasm.

"Maybe we were looking at the wrong place," Patrick added, swiveling his entire body around in circles as he took in the landscape. "Back in March we didn't know where we wanted to go, but we always wanted to see Alaska, and man, am I glad we came."

"Back in March," George said as he started the truck, "you were lucky you could see the island. It was still winter up here, the trees were bare and the ground was still covered with snow."

We pulled out of the parking lot and headed toward town on the only road that went east or west, passing by Boy Scout Lake, driving up over a small hill and then around into Deadman's

Curve. George swung the truck into the viewing area and slowed to a stop. We all tumbled out and stood in awe, taking in the panoramic view of the ocean dotted with small green islands, and a few fishing boats scattered at their favorite fishing places or coming in with their catch of the day.

More Wows, Oh wows, and Oh My Gods emitted from the visitors as a bald eagle glided by, wings stretched wide and head bent towards them as if to offer his own welcome.

They remarked on the quiet town with no traffic jams, sirens, horns honking, or shouting crowds. Kodiak was a peaceful fishing village. No Iceland Truckers out here. If more than five cars passed on the road it was considered rush hour; if more than two people were at a river it was a crowd, and sirens were rare since most locals knew how to take care of themselves. The cameras came out, pictures were taken, and then we drove back through town and out towards Monashka Bay. We passed Fort Abercrombie State Park, a World War II historical site and small museum, which displayed period artifacts, turret guns, and bunkers used long ago against the anticipated invasion of Japanese military. The blacktop road meandered around the hillside, through tall trees and overgrown alder bushes that hung close to the roadsides. Driving on the narrow gray path, flanked by a thick canopy of foliage felt like hiking through the woods, as we cruised higher up to the dirt road turnoff, and finally, home.

Late the next morning, after the visitors caught up with the inevitable jet lag, the four of us went into town to the local sports store and purchased the required fishing licenses and then to the "super" market to pick up some food supplies. Then we headed over to the Buskin River for tryouts.

Salmon started out from a frozen lake in the early spring, swam down the river and out into the salty ocean. After a few years, if they survived the many predators at sea, they made their way back up through the same river to spawn and die. This was survival of the fastest, smartest, and most learned, going back to the beginning of time.

The weather played a major factor in any vacation. Kodiak was no exception. It rained at a steady pace for the next three days, putting a damper on an ocean voyage, so we kept to the rivers or cruised through the neighborhoods pointing out historical sites and local specialty places like Kodiak's own brewery.

On the fourth day, the dark clouds moved on and the gray sky turned lighter by the minute, like a dimmer switch slowly moving the sun up from the horizon.

"Hand me that anchor and line over there." George pointed at the pile in the corner of the garage from his high perch on the eighteen-foot metal cabin cruiser. It was just cracking dawn at 4:30 in the morning and George liked to get an early start. Jake and Patrick dutifully hauled anchor and line, then ice chests, fishing rods, and buckets of bait up to George with sleepy, clumsy gestures and half-stifled yawns.

"The tide's just right and we want to get out there and catch some fish," I said, following the men, arms loaded with coffee thermoses and two smaller ice chests packed with sandwiches and snacks.

"But the birds aren't even up yet," protested Patrick, rubbing his eyes with the back of his hand.

"Neither are the fish," George said with twinkling eyes as he arranged the gear into various nooks and crannies. "So we're gonna catch 'em by surprise."

"Cool," Jake said, coming awake with eager excitement. "I hope we sneak up on a big one." And so we did. George caught the first halibut, then Jake caught the next two and finally, when we had all but given up for the day, Patrick caught a nice eighty-pounder and I caught a respectable-sized sea bass. The laughter and bantering continued well after dinner that night as we recounted every detail.

After a few more such lucky days on the water, it was time for Patrick and Jake to depart, or so stated their airplane itineraries. George and I stood at the patio window looking out with decreasing optimism.

"What do you think, George?" I queried with a frown.

"Positive thinking, Clare, positive thinking." George wore a frown, too as he looked out over the hillside. Fog had rolled in. Thick and pale gray, it covered the island, totally obscuring our once picturesque view of field and forest and ocean. For that matter, we couldn't see to the other side of our driveway. No wind dared to budge the smothering glob that cast an eerie muffled silence over the land.

It was said that the Japanese had made their escape in such weather during World War II from an island in the Aleutian Chain that stretched just northwest of Kodiak. American pilots could not see through the heavy fog and thick cloud cover and when it finally lifted, some of the Japanese troops had made their getaway in a waiting ship. Those who remained later perished in the ensuing war.

Fog on the deck meant all activity ceased. No flying, no fishing, no hiking, just stop where you were. Those not used to this sort of thing became anxious and severely distraught. To those who'd paid a king's ransom to get here, or those with pressing demands to return home, the disappointment was tough to hide.

We made fruitless efforts to keep up lagging spirits and worked diligently at finding things to keep their minds otherwise occupied, but nobody could change the weather. The tiny airport became crowded with disgruntled passengers and ticket agents became short tempered as we carted fish boxes, luggage and visitors back and forth from home to airport twice a day for three days with little hope a plane would land.

On the fourth day, Mother Nature relented and early morning brought the long-awaited clear skies and sunshine. Everyone was relieved and we said goodbye to our friends as they finally boarded the plane.

Our next set of visitors was not so amiable. Nor did they listen very well. George's brother arrived with a friend of dubious character and an arrogance that boded ill with George. Still, the visit started with friendly overtures before the disasters came.

"Betcha I can climb up and down that mountain in two hours flat," boasted Doug, pointing to Barometer Mountain. He was a large man and appeared physically fit, but George tried to warn his brother with stories of past fatal incidents. Not to be deterred, he began the hike.

The best thing about Barometer Mountain, rising over 2,500 feet into the clouds, was the well-worn path that parted the thick vegetation, allowing clear visibility for much of the way along the steep incline. The worst was that it was much tougher than it looked from down below.

Doug returned after six long anxious hours in a seriously disheveled state with numerous scratches and cuts, shredded clothes, and panting with great gasps of exhaustion. I feared a heart attack as he collapsed to the ground at our feet.

"Water," was the only thing he mumbled, like some shriveled man in a desert movie. I quickly handed him a glassful, then poured another when it emptied into his parched mouth. George shook his head and went about finding bandages and a clean set of clothes. Doug stumbled into the house, stood under the hot shower and after George applied first aid, crawled into bed.

A few days later, we lost his companion. We had met with a group of friends at Pasagshak State Park, about an hour's drive south of Kodiak. It was a favorite location for locals and tourists alike as the mouth of a large river opened to the ocean, providing ample fishing with great rewards. It was a scenic vista of tree-stunted rolling mountains covered with thick vegetation forming a U shape around the bay. Thin waterfalls cascaded down steep ravines cut into the low valley in the center. Gray rocky cliffs dropped down to the ocean at unexpected intervals.

George suddenly looked around the crowd in curious dismay. He walked over to his brother. "Doug, where's Dennis?" George asked.

"Don't know, he was here a while ago. Probably wandered off somewhere. He does that sometimes." Doug shrugged and casually glanced around. He spotted the ice chest containing the beer and walked in that direction, leaving George standing alone.

I noted the stormy look on George's face and walked over to him. "What's up?" I queried, following the direction of his face as he scanned the hillsides.

"Dennis wandered off God knows where." George stepped over to his truck and took out the binoculars. He carefully searched for anything moving in the thick bush but to no avail. He lowered the lenses, still eyeing the landscape, and took in a deep breath. "Shit," George said, and stomped over to Doug while I followed in his angry wake.

George had a low tolerance for stupidity and an even lower tolerance for people who didn't listen. He felt a personal responsibility for animals and people alike, shooing deer from the busy roadway or yelling a warning to anglers at the rivers when he spotted a bear in close proximity. And now Dennis was nowhere to be seen.

"How long has he been gone?" George interrogated Doug. "Which direction did he go?" Doug had no idea.

"Maybe he'll come back in a little while," I said hopefully. "Maybe we could just wait for him."

"No time to wait," George said as he noted the darkening skies headed for our sobering party. "We need to find him now. Scatter out everybody." In rapid response, everyone walked hurriedly in different directions calling out for Dennis. Some drove their trucks to the very end of the road, honking horns and flashing headlights. Others hopped on four-wheelers and zipped across the boggy terrain, shouting and whistling. Dogs ran after them, joining the search. Another half hour, the wind lifting his cap from his head, black clouds climbing swiftly down the mountains from the east, George made up his mind. "We need help," he said to the group.

Someone volunteered to drive back to town and in a record two hours brought back a professional rescue team of eleven people and four highly trained German shepherds. Each member, including the dogs was wearing blaze orange vests specially made to guard against injuries from thorns and poisonous cow parsnip, known by locals as poochki, which could cause a nasty red skin rash similar to poison ivy.

George gave a description of Dennis, as his brother, now duly caught up in the seriousness of the situation, stood by his side and provided further details.

The rescue team pulled out maps, compasses, and binoculars along with their own safety gear, discussed a quick plan, and nodded with familiar gestures of agreement. George and Doug, and I piled more driftwood onto the small campfire. In the growing dusk, it would become a beacon for the improvised "command center."

Into the rain-drenched howling night they methodically searched, reported, and searched again. It wasn't until early the next morning that Dennis was found. We watched four members of the rescue team bring him gingerly down the side of a hill, pushing through thick alder bushes, skirting around trees, and wading through tall, choking weeds. He lay in a makeshift stretcher, carried by two people, while two others cleared a path.

The expert dogs had sniffed him out where he lay crunched in a crevice after he had stumbled and fallen late the previous day. The lucky man escaped with only a sprained ankle, broken wrist, and several scrapes and bruises, along with mild hypothermia. He offered no excuses for himself as he hobbled through the airport and onto the plane. Doug said a sheepish goodbye to George and gave me a brief hug, then followed his companion.

The first set of visitors for the following year arrived just in time for the whales. From mid-April to mid-May, the giant mammals migrated north to Alaskan waters from the California coast. Like huge locomotives cresting a hill, their dark shiny bodies pushed the water aside as they heaved themselves up to the surface in long, slow motion, spewing great plumes of steamlike watery spray high into the air. With surprising grace

the mammoth creatures dove back into the ocean depths, dragging their long bodies across the surface and down with a final
wave of their fan-shaped tails, dripping silvery waterfalls before
they too disappeared beneath the surface.

Whale breaching near Buoy 4

Whale Fest was a popular pastime during this period, and
everyone got into the excitement of this annual event because it
signaled the arrival of spring. The local radio station announced
whale sightings as people spotted these ocean monsters and
called in the locations. People from everywhere rushed to the
various viewing spots with binoculars and cameras to catch a
glimpse of these majestic creatures. Whales arrived to feed on
the plentiful array of fish, other sea mammals, and plankton
found around the cooler Kodiak waters.

Maggie, Connie, George and I stood with Jerry on his boat
looking in the direction he pointed. We swayed in unison slightly
as the giant whale's wake nudged against the small boat. Maggie
and Connie hailed from Anchorage, where they were longtime
residents and longtime friends of ours. Neither had been on a

fishing boat in the ocean before and each marveled at the smells, sights, and sounds as we motored around the shores spotting puffins, sea lions, and eagles.

These ladies were true Alaskans - strong, independent, and lively with excited chatter. They insisted on baiting their own hooks, much to Jerry's relief, and teased him mercilessly. Both women were in their late thirties, one blond, the other brunette, stylish and sophisticated in their city ways, witty and cheerful and fun to have around.

They found humor in most situations, including an engine fire on their most recent trip. A frayed wire had caused flames to erupt at the rear of the boat. Jerry ran around the deck frantically flapping his arms and shoving things out of the way, barking orders while George calmly hosed it out with the dry chemical extinguisher and then fixed the faulty wire. All the while, Maggie and Connie sat inside the cabin with me and cheered the men on, our knights in shining armor.

Visitors were a welcome respite for most locals. Relatives and friends descended upon Kodiak throughout summer and well into fall. Alaska was fast becoming a popular new tourist destination.

Visitors brought a pleasant break especially to fishermen's wives, who tended to be lonely at times during the commercial fishing season. This special group of women waited weeks and sometimes months for their commercial anglers to return. They maintained their houses and families and dealt with the problems of broken faucets or grinding car engines, or sick children, or birthing babies, or vicious blizzards by themselves.

They maintained the home base for the captain and crew and took care of the necessities of the fishing business while the others were gone. The wives knew almost as much about generators, engines, and hydraulic fluids as the fishermen themselves, simply because when something happened out there, the spouse generally ordered the parts, lined up the repair appointments, and arranged supply deliveries to the nearest location of the boat.

Theses patient, strong spirited women carefully nurtured a network of like-minded individuals by volunteering for church events or local charities. A few women even compiled a cook-book, *Memoirs of a Galley Slave*, with recipes worthy of any gourmet restaurant that specialized in preparing, processing, and cooking the bounty of the sea. They kept busy with their chosen activities, but one could observe the worry and weariness concealed just under the surface when the weather changed from calm to stormy seas.

A strong sense of camaraderie endured through generations of waiting and watching, of being the stay-at-home part of this most hazardous occupation. It became especially notable when they quickly circled around in support of a widow in her time of need. Each knew it could happen to any one of them, as they mingled at a wake and softly comforted each other, torn between sorrow and jubilance. They prepared food, assisted with servic-es, and ensured names of the lost were remembered during the Fisherman's Memorial Service held each year on Memorial Day.

Visitors of a different sort began arriving in Kodiak in 2006. With the increase in Alaskan tourism, huge cruise ships laden with more than one thousand tourists docked at the Port of Kodiak, bringing a much needed boost to the economy. These visitors came in answer to the colorful brochures and advertise-ments aptly depicting the beauty of Alaska in general and Kodiak Island as a must-see destination on their itineraries.

Visitors of several nationalities, some with heavy accents, strolled single file down the gangway, clicking away with cell phones and miniature cameras, huddled into light jackets ill-suited for the cool weather of the North. Still, they seemed pleased with our Emerald Isle in all its summer glory of green mountains, colorful wildflowers, and rivers of leaping fish pur-sued by giant brown bears. They marveled at numerous bald eagles posing in treetops, or light poles, or corners of cannery buildings. Kodiak boasted up to eight cruise ships in a season, sporting huge shimmering white bows and colorful Norwegian Cruise emblems. Kodiak was drifting towards tourism – like it or not.

George and I sat in the truck one day on the side of the road opposite the Port of Kodiak. We were stunned at the enormous size of the elegant cruise ship and watched a group of visitors strolling towards our "downtown" area, chattering in a language we did not understand. *What did they think of our island? Did they see what I saw? Did they feel the wildness, the calm, the quiet spirit of the place?*

Most of our friends and relatives spoke pleasantly about their visits up here, but was it out of friendly respect to their hosts or truly felt? We often observed smiles and excited comments during their brief visits, but I supposed we would never really know. After all, we were never visitors. We came to be residents and plowed into this place with all the backbreaking, mind-boggling, stubborn tenacity we could muster. It was all worth it, I had decided. Well, there were *those* times.

16 RUNNING WITH BEARS

They were huge! Not that I've seen any small bears, but viewed from close range, like our backyard, the perspective was large and the bears appeared even larger. To see such magnificent animals in all their natural glory was to behold heaven on earth. To see them marching towards my porch was scary.

It was five o'clock in the morning when the neighbor's dog woke us up barking nonstop. Midnight, the black and white Malamute mix who lived about fifty yards from our bedroom window, usually barked at most things but this time the tone was different.

A dog's bark carried different meanings. For example, a small short "yip yip" means hello, or a "yark, yark, yark" means someone is walking past or coming to visit. This bark was a low, deep excited warning bark that definitely meant intruders.

George and I flipped upright in bed at the same time and peered out of the bedroom window. Sleepy turned to awake and then fully awake in the span of fifteen seconds. We spotted the two large, dark forms moving through the tall grasses and alder bushes, at a sauntering pace. They prowled down the path, worn down by countless dog walks, four-wheeler treks, and deer hooves, moving their heads from side to side, as if searching.

And they were. The fish were late coming back into the rivers once again. U.S. Fish and Wildlife had closed the nearby rivers to all fishing due to the slow arrival of red salmon. No fish in the rivers meant that bears would have to find other sustenance. They made their way through residential neighborhoods, breaking into sheds, pickup trucks, and dumpsters, searching for food.

As they made their way towards our house, we quickly thought of anything they might catch a scent of that we had erroneously left outside, but we knew we had put everything away, cleaned up any scraps of food on the barbeque grill from the night before and locked up the fish totes securely out of reach. Still, they kept coming closer.

George and I scurried to the patio door for a full view. I had thoughts of fear mixed with wonder as the bears padded up the small hill appearing on the path only a few yards from the deck. With only fuzzy thoughts regarding anything but danger, George ran through the house and over to the guesthouse. Our newest visitor, Jack, was sleeping off jet lag and hadn't heard the racket.

"Jack. Jack, get the fireworks, hurry, we got bears!" yelled George as he banged through the door and tossed bags and boxes around looking for the caps left over from our celebration the night before. "The sound will scare them away," George shouted over his shoulder at Jack.

Jack threw back his sleeping bag and jumped up in terror.

"Bears? What bears, Where? What are you talking about? What fireworks?" He joined George in a blur of frantic running around, arms flying and excited yelling about the bears and where they put the fireworks.

Together they raced outside towards the path in the high grasses and began lighting off the fireworks. That George and Jack were doing all this in their underwear was shocking enough, but the ear popping racket roused neighbors from several houses, not just to dogs barking, doors slamming and fireworks blasting, but to two men in their briefs in the middle of the yard shouting at the bears.

The whole commotion lasted less than five minutes, but the effect on the neighbors, the two men, and most likely the two bears, was comical and awe-inspiring and made a good story for years to come. I had a new respect for these awesome creatures—the bears, not the half-naked men— and even felt a bit sorry for them for having to scrounge through people's garbage, face off with barking dogs, strange men, and loud cracks of light.

The bears scampered swiftly into the woods, the neighbors went back into their houses and I hoped the fish would show up soon. George stomped back into the house and pounced back in bed. "Now maybe I can get some sleep around here," he grumbled as he pulled the blankets over his head.

Bearly Noticed

Lucky enjoying his favorite pastime

17 IT'S A DOG'S TOWN

Kodiak was dog country. Most everyone had a dog of one breed or another. The predominant breed was the Black Labrador or Golden Retriever. They sat patiently in vehicles, watching people come and go into the post office or into the grocery store. They stood courageously on the bows of large commercial fishing vessels or small wobbly skiffs with dignified balance and grace. They participated in every aspect of life on this remote mysterious island with an abundance of energy and curiosity. Whether it was sunny, stormy, windy, or foggy, they traveled with their human companions ready to meet the challenge of the day. Kodiak dogs were not only constant companions and lively entertainment; they were protectors of property and person, especially from bears.

We had raised three such large black Labs over the years, their smooth shiny coats wet with rain or speckled with white flakes of snow as they plunged their heads into the fluffy white drifts in search of I don't know what, a long ago buried bone or stick or ball.

Blackie was our first, arriving with me from Colorado by car and airplane. He was by far the smartest dog we had ever known. Blackie seemed to know English perfectly, just couldn't speak a word of it. He was tall and proud, carried his head high with knowledge and instinct way beyond our expectations.

We acquired "Blackie's Worst Nightmare" as a present from George's dad one blustery February night. A pedigree Lab, Blackie's Worst Nightmare (as registered with the American Kennel Club) was so named because as a puppy he tended to pester the mature eight-year-old who thought he was the head of the household. Blackie taught Nightmare all the right things, though, and kept him at tail's length, letting him know when his behavior was unacceptable.

Nightmare learned well and grew up to become a good-natured dog with exceptional courage. He strolled around the neighborhood (despite the many methods of restraint we tried), where everyone loved him as he played the role of meet-and-greet like the best politician. He was friendly to all creatures large and small, and knew every tree and bush within miles. Nightmare was a wanderer. As much as we tried to restrain him, he would deftly find escape routes, ducking under fences, dragging around anchors and invariably sneaking off into any direction. These Houdini disappearances drove us into states of panic as we searched endlessly into the wee hours of the night and morning trying to find him.

He would suddenly appear at the door just when we had almost given up any hope. A most exasperating dog at times, but we loved his congenial nature. He found the neighbors' missing dog one day when they came over to us while we were in the yard stacking wood. George turned to Nightmare and simply told him to "Go find Rocket." Ten minutes later, Nightmare came back with Rocket, a small Yorkshire terrier, following gratefully behind him, clearly lost in the nearby woods and now happy to be with his owner again.

The pied piper of the hilltop won respect and plenty of biscuits from neighbors and friends. Visitors wanted his company at night and neighboring dogs clamored for his company during the day. His natural instinct was to chase rabbits, but once he caught up with them, he would gently lick the worn-out creatures until they caught their breath and gingerly hopped away.

Once we came home from a long day of fishing to find him on the back porch with a mouse nestled against his soft underbelly, both of them snoozing peacefully. But he was a serious protector as well, alerting us to any strange noise or unfamiliar car pulling into the driveway. His bark was loud and deep until he recognized the intruder or until we did. He got along well with most people with few exceptions. Those few knew instantly and never returned. Nightmare was large for a Lab, with a big heart and enormous courage. I felt completely safe with Nightmare whenever George was away.

One night, Nightmare ran a bear off the deck that stood only a few feet from my patio door. Around the yard they went, bear chasing annoying barking dog, until Nightmare deftly outwitted the bear, by circling a large clump of trees and running for the other door. I slammed it shut after he raced through, and we both watched the bear, still down in the yard searching for his antagonist.

Blackie's Worst Nightmare

Nightmare, in turn, taught Lucky all his tricks. Lucky was a rescue puppy transported via airfreight from Anchorage by a friend who couldn't stand letting his neighbor put the puppy in the pound once he departed the state. Lucky was crated and loaded onto the plane for the one-hour flight to Kodiak.

Nine hours and four airports later, Lucky had finally arrived. Circumstances, from mechanical failures to crew substitutes to flight changes delayed his arrival until at last, we were notified that our puppy had arrived in Kodiak. The dog accumulated more flight miles that trip than I had in a year.

Nightmare, by then in his prime, took the young pup around to his favorite sites disappearing for hours. We were seriously distraught on one such occasion when the two dogs had not returned by nightfall. At 6 a.m. a woman called from several miles away asking if we owned a small black lab. Fortunately, he wore a green dog-paw tag with his name and our phone number.

In another instance, the two runaways were spotted on the top of Pillar Mountain enjoying the picnickers, who offered hot dogs, marshmallows, and various other handouts. By the time we drove up there, the pair had disappeared and by the time we got back to the house, they had reappeared on the porch with sore paws, stuffed tummies, and tongues almost touching the ground. That was Lucky's last trip with Nightmare. He decided he didn't like leaving home. He became my shadow. Whatever had happened out there, he wanted no more of it. He patiently sat at the door after that day, and waited to be escorted for his walks.

The three Labs were all wonderful dogs; each had his own personality and different requirements and different antics. Blackie was intelligent and dependable, Nightmare was courageous and congenial, Lucky was athletic beyond proportions and by far the most vocal. He howled with the radio, groaned at the slightest behavior correction, and always huffed and puffed until he got the attention he thought he deserved. And he was a serious stickler for routine.

While most people knew to have a battery operated alarm clock as a backup due to frequent power outages on the island, we had three. My alarm clock rang first, then George's second, and if that didn't work, there was Lucky. At seven years old, he had become the current taskmaster, who kept us on a strict routine like a steady stopwatch.

Exactly sixty seconds before my alarm clock rang he would position himself on the floor on my side of the bed, and begin the "Labrador stare." Lucky stared at me with such intensity that it actually woke me up.

At first, he just stared quietly and waited. After the second time I had hit the snooze button, he began the paw shift. At fifteen-second intervals, he shifted his weight from one paw to the other making enough noise to make a soft thump. He stared and waited, then shifted his paws. Right paw, thump. Left paw, thump. This paw shifting continued until George's alarm clock rang. If we didn't stir, he stared, waited, and then thumped his paws at steady intervals. Stared, waited, and shifted paws. It was now five minutes past his interpretation of snooze and that's when Lucky got impatient.

He started with a short shake of fur. Very brief, not a full-length shake, just enough to cause a slight jingle of his collar as the metal pet tags clinked together. However, we were not ready yet. We were not anxious to start the day at five a.m. The automatic coffeepot had just started and the aroma was soothing, the blankets were warm, the sheets soft. We needed just a few more minutes…that we wouldn't get.

Backup alarm clocks worked. They gave you those few extra minutes, but you couldn't ignore them forever. Lucky wouldn't be ignored. As a self-appointed third backup alarm clock, the quiet stare, the patient wait, the shifting paws, the gentle jingle of collar turned into an all out backup alarm clock blare!

Lucky began his famous 50,000 fleas act. No small thing, this act, it quickly became a floor shaking, foot scratching, collar twisting, loud moaning attack on himself like he was battling 50,000 fleas that tormented his whole body. The noise was horrendous, the fur flew in all directions, and the bed shook like an earthquake!

I finally opened my eyes. His solemn look of surprise was almost genuine. His studied expression of "Oh, I'm sorry, did I wake you? It's these fleas, you see," was classic. "Knock it off," I hissed. "We don't have fleas in Kodiak." One of the great things about owning a pet in Kodiak was the absence of fleas. If the pet was born here, it never had fleas. If it was brought here from anywhere else, the fleas quickly died. They couldn't survive the cold climate. Alas, a backup alarm clock worked. Ours just happened to be a very effective Lab, who had artfully learned the 50,000 fleas act.

Dogs played a prominent role in the Kodiak lifestyle. We had raised, trained, and loved all three of our Labs and they in turn brought us so much joy. I liked to think they were happy here on our hilltop. I would lay awake at night sometimes, and listen to the comforting sound of dogs barking in the distance, like night watchmen signaling the "all is well." First one, then another, then another would join in - a chorus of dogs singing good night to the stars, and to me.

Rising Tide at Chiniak Bay

18 TREE SMART

It was that season again, late in September, and time to set up our winter's supply of firewood. By then we had things easier with the help of a newly purchased Model 843 Bobcat, a mechanical workhorse that saved us countless hours and sore muscles. Despite the desire to continue the do-it-yourself life-style, we were beginning to feel our age creeping up on us.

We hoisted the last tree up from the gully and sat down on a stump for a much-needed break. A local sawyer left a few logs for us after clearing the next lot for a large house soon to be built. The tall, straight spruce trees, already limbed, ranged from thirty to sixty feet long and some were almost forty-two inches in diameter. The clearing looked out of place up here on the side of the mountain, but progress was moving on.

The logs had lain there for a full year before we could get to them. Now that the fall frost had removed most of the thick vegetation and killed the poochki and thorny devil's club, we could safely climb down into the tangles of alder trees, weeds, and brush. George double-wrapped the two-inch chain around the widest part of the tree and I wrapped another length of chain at the other end. We each dragged our end of the chain and met at the Bobcat. George clipped each one to the front bollard, climbed up into the machine and worked the levers to haul the logs up from the ravine.

We sat on a log and jokingly pondered what people in the big cities did for fun. Although this was backbreaking labor, we welcomed the diversion from the overwhelming, stressful workday. Logging, chopping, and stacking wood was a good workout and provided a sense of accomplishment, not to mention a necessity for our winter heat.

When we first found this lot on the side of the mountain overlooking Monashka Bay, it was surrounded by woods and littered with all kinds of animal tracks from rabbits, fox, and deer, and of course, bear. We gradually relaxed and marveled at their stealthy, trepid ways.

It was late afternoon and George had gone back to the house for refreshments and more gas for the Bobcat. I called to the dogs and decided to hike into the woods. My mind drifted along as I gazed around, smelling the piney breath on the light breeze.

Sitka spruce trees stuck up out of the ground like bunches of pipe cleaners, their shallow roots barely holding on to the sandy ash-covered earth. I tipped my head back and followed one tree to its top, amazed at the height and strength of the thing. I touched the gray scaly bark, lightly draped in a mossy wool gown.

I wondered if I would want to live like a tree— sure, growth would be slower each year, but people would look up to me in awe for a while and I would look vibrant and pretty forever as the years drifted by. Of course, someone would buy up the land where I stood. The land where my roots had grasped tentatively at first, then persistently for so many years, would shake and quake from bulldozers, caterpillars, and graders clearing the area. Next thing I knew a chainsaw would cut me down. Maybe not like a tree.

Trees were proud, I had thought as I continued on. They reached for the sky every day of their lives. They didn't stop growing—they didn't stop providing protection and food and warmth to the many critters like the shiny black ravens and chee-chee birds and red belly wrens that fluttered in and out among their outstretched branches, along with the squirrels, who built tiny nests into small cracks in the bark. The trees protected those petite little chatterers that scurried up and down the tree trunks in quick, nervous movements, starting then stopping, going someplace, from tree to tree.

Trees made a lofty perch for the elegant bald eagles with their pure white feathered heads, shouting to each other in their regal chirps to all the world below. I watched an eagle launch from a branch bending it down as the great bird spread its giant wings and took flight. I followed it upwards as it soared in spiraling circles, curling up and up, then swooped down quickly, making a perfect landing on another branch, as a pilot landed his plane - smoothly, talons out, wings back, flapping slightly, then gracefully dropping and folding onto the sturdy branch of the tree.

The branches formed a kind of ladder, perfect for climbing quickly if a bear came down the path. I glanced around warily as I noticed the telltale signs that a bear had recently passed this way. The bear had stopped at the tree and rubbed an itchy patch of hide, maybe just that morning. The tree had yielded a fraction at the top, swaying slightly, dropping needles to the ground. Hunks of brown, fuzzy fur stuck to the bark about eye level. I was sure the bear had not missed it. The bear's coat was thick and several inches long.

Spruce trees were beautiful, provided protection, made a nice scratching post, and even lifeless, they were still useful. Trees could also hurt you.

I walked with my dogs farther into the woods, entering just across the road and climbing up the narrow ditch. I pulled myself up the other side by grabbing alder branches lining the dirt road. Blackie and Nightmare darted across and up the other side along with me, sniffing at the various animal scents and foliage and heading toward the well-worn game trail that meandered around and up to the other side of the mountain.

The trail was familiar, yet we had discovered something interesting each trip, like a new kind of wildflower, tightly curled ferns, ripening salmonberries, blueberries, and ground berries, or a tiny new fledging spruce twig, trying its hardest to grow as big and tall as the overshadowing adult trees surrounding it. In the silence of the woods, we walked on, listening to squirrels chatter, chee chee birds twill and ravens squawk out their whereabouts to each other.

We climbed passed the same scenery of stately old trees and rocks and dead branches and decrepit logs, lumped on the ground, covered with fuzzy green lichen. We eagerly navigated the path, weaving around small bushes and half-buried rocks. As the earth kept moving, we tried to catch up with it, moving forward and upward, the goal was to get to the top.

The trail leveled off to a carpeted meadow of mossy green lichen cut into the side of the mountain. The three of us broke into a run, dodging trees, leaping over logs, and swerving around the bulky bushes, racing each other to the other side. It was exhilarating and fun, as a sense of urgency pulled us onward.

We raced to the edge of the clearing, and then back again, and on down the hillside. The agile dogs leaped and bounced ahead of me faster and faster, the downward direction increased the speed and I plummeted out of control.

Too late, I realized there was no need to rush. Nature was always there. The forest, with all its creatures, bushes, and plants that blurred passed at freight train speed, stood ready to be enjoyed forever. It was better, I suddenly realized, to take it at a slower pace. Besides, like running with scissors in your hand, running downhill in a forest was hazardous.

Thoughts vaporized into the clouds – a surreal, not unpleasant experience as my body flew through the air. The serene beauty of the forest, rich textures of bark on trees, smooth thin branches of alder bushes, tiny blades of grass drifted passed in a dreamlike state. I was falling through the clouds, falling and rolling awkwardly down to earth, hitting with full force into blackness.

I woke from my daze with two dogs, one lapped gently on the right side of my face. My left side pressed hard into the earth. The other dog sat upright, like a sentinel, ever guarding feebleminded me. My shoulder was unnaturally bent inwards under my body, one leg stayed uphill; the other was twisted sharply, with the knee ground deeply into the damp mossy soil. I lay there for a few more minutes, trying to get my scattered, painful thoughts reorganized. Blackie nudged closer against my back and Nightmare stopped licking and peered into my eyes.

I struggled to heave myself up to a sitting position, white-hot pain shot through my body from my shoulder down my back, and into my legs. I wiggled my fingers and decided the shoulder was dislocated from the socket it was supposed to reside in, but thankfully not broken. I glared back at the log, where the fuzzy green lichen had masked a stout appendage about three inches long. It stuck up purposely to catch my pant leg.

With aching effort, I pushed myself to a standing position and checked for any other abnormalities about my body. My shirtsleeve was ripped down to the cuff, exposing bloody abrasions on my elbow, and another ragged tear at my knee oozed blood through chunks of dirt and rocks. I gently flexed ankles, back, and neck with no further stabs of pain and limped slowly back down the trail. The dogs marched on either side of me and graciously ignored my humiliating moment.

The cleared lot next to ours gradually turned into a beautiful house and neighbors moved to our hill. Two more lots were cleared a few years later, and more houses were under construction. George and I watched with mixed feelings of excitement about meeting new friends, and regret at losing what we had come to think of as our quiet backyard forest.

Heavy equipment arrived, trees savagely cut down, and wide gashes gouged out of the hillsides made way for spiraling driveways and large beautiful houses with ocean views. Although the new houses were more than a hundred feet away, it seemed that our once-peaceful hill would become another suburban development. We cringed at the encroachment. We frowned in dismay, and sighed at our loss.

Logging truck making way for neighbors

We soon discovered that these country neighbors cherished the same peace and quiet we did, and friendships grew. It became a comfort when things went wrong to have someone in near proximity. Intrusions were immediately discussed, whether bears, burglars, or bad teenagers, and we all watched each other, including our pets and dwellings, notifying each other by phone or a visit if something didn't seem normal.

Like the call that George answered at four in the morning when a neighbor heard loud rustling noises close to his back porch. George jumped out of bed and rushed over to the patio door that faced the neighbors' porch at an angle. He switched on his mega spotlight and shone it in the direction of the porch. It was partially concealed by a large bush that shook and rattled against the stairwell.

George stepped out onto the deck, peered closer into the night and then called out to the rustling noisemaker. "Hey!" At once, the rustling stopped and the big head turned around. Its antlers became clearly visible in the spotlight. The large buck was apparently scraping off the velvet from its protruding rack of horns. "Get," was George's next command and the deer promptly obeyed. It warily stepped away from the porch, sauntered down the short hill, and trotted off into the night.

"It was a big buck, Al, nothing to worry about, it's gone now." George spoke into the phone. "No bear this time."

We came to rely on each other, snow-plowing each other's driveways, pulling each other's vehicles out of ditches on cold snowy nights, and sharing quiet dinners and lively picnics at each other's houses. It made the inevitable even more difficult.

Afognak Cabin 2006

19 CABIN CACHE

George and I sat on the deck of our newly constructed 16 by 20 feet cabin on Afognak Island. Coffee cups warmed our hands as we watched the sun slowly rise above Whale Island, across the bay.

In August 2001 we'd purchased the 40 acres of land, site unseen. An ad in the newspaper from the BLM announced a bid sale for remote land. We submitted the necessary paperwork along with our earnest money and hoped for the best. Four months later, we received the notice in the mail: we were the proud owners of a remote piece of land on Afognak Island.

We launched our small skiff with a map in hand and motored the 20 minutes from Anton Larsen Bay, across the Kizhuyak Bay, over the choppy water beyond Whale Pass. We plowed past Hog Island, which really did look like a hog, complete with a snout of a cliff sticking out to the north, and into a shallow bay littered with dangerous hidden reefs.

Fortunately, it was high tide and our shallow-bottomed boat glided easily to the beach. We grabbed the bow, hauled it farther up the beach, turned to a ledge of grassy bank and made the climb. The ocean front property backed up to Litnik Mountain with an abandoned church on one side and a graveyard on the other. Dense grassy fields scattered with colorful wildflowers and giant spruce trees with green fuzzy arms, welcomed us to the island. About a hundred feet inland a small lake circled by alders and more tall grass completed the peaceful scene. Ducks glided gracefully across to the far side and a beaver slapped its tail on the water with a disgruntled air at being thus disturbed. Seagulls soared overhead, looking down at us with quizzical beady eyes. Two shiny black ravens squawked from a nearby tree, announcing our arrival.

We found a couple of tree stumps, laid our backpacks down and gazed wondrously at this remote site, excited to be the proud owners of such breathtaking beauty. This was it. This was what we had dreamed of - owning a piece of the rock and a small lake to boot! We looked at each other and smiled broadly, turning again to the sea, taking in the panoramic view of watery horizon, gauzy mountainous islands in the distance, and our own sandy beach that stretched to low-lying hills on either side.

Before the earthquake of 1964, this section of the island was the site of the Afognak Native village. We had researched the area after the acquisition and became intrigued by the history of the inhabitants. An archeological dig was in progress farther along the beach and a small community of self-sufficient Russian descendants lived about three miles to the west. On the other side of the island, a logging operation harvested timber from the area that was shipped to faraway places such as Japan and China.

But this small parcel was ours, at least for now. George believed we only rented the space, wherever we were, and then we died, and it went back to Mother Nature, or someone else rented it for a while. I liked that thought. When it was time to leave, it somehow made it seem easier.

Two years later on a cool summer day in July 2003, we finished loading the landing barge with supplies, lumber, plywood, windows, shingles, paint, nails, and personal stuff such as food, rain gear, and extra clothing.

Conrad, the carpenter who had accepted the small but logistically challenging cabin project and two locals, Lenny and Tommy, helped us load the supplies. It took seven trips and three months to complete our dream cabin, with no catastrophes other than one broken window and a few bumps, bruises, and abrasions.

It was perfect. We spent the first night stretched out on canvas cots, piled with sleeping bags, pillows, and enough blankets to smother a horse. George kept the small woodstove alive by feeding it every two hours, and the cabin stayed cozy all night.

An early morning walk down the beach with Lucky revealed the fresh tracks of a bear traveling toward the small salmon creek to the east. Silly not to think about bears being in the area, but it had come as a surprise. From then on, we ventured out of the cabin with caution and full assortment of bear deterrents such as pepper spray, whistles, and a weapon of some sort. Even trips to the handsomely decorated outhouse required due diligence with safety precautions. It was a testament to the bears, however, that we never actually saw one around the cabin during the whole time we stayed there. In fact, we saw more bears in town than we did at our remote site cabin. They left plenty of signs, but they seemed to keep to themselves, as did we.

The cabin started as a one-room open area with a deck on opposite ends. Later we closed in both decks and made a kitchen area in the front and a storage room in the back. The middle space became a sleeping area at night and a nice sitting room during the day. We added a deck to the left side where we sat and watched the sun rise and set.

"Clare, listen." George whispered one morning as he pointed to the thin yellow curve of the rising sun. "It's so quiet you can hear the sun rise." I laughed at his little joke, but it was not hard to imagine after that. It would be a soft quiet sound as it grew larger and larger, climbing up slowly, turning the dark sky to gray, then rosy pink, and then to a luminous blue-white as it reached above the water and pushed the waves gently toward the beach.

We spent many long relaxing weekends at our cabin, making driftwood tables and tree stump chairs. We arranged stores of food in black plastic milk crates hauled over on the skiff along with supplies of fresh water and other necessities.

Each spring, however, we had found the inside of the outhouse destroyed. Shredded toilet paper piled knee deep with twigs, moss, dead leaves, and what looked like bird feathers tumbled out of the plywood door onto the feet of the first person to enter. Squirrels had spent the winter in the outhouse nesting cozily in piles of shredded toilet paper. No matter how hard George tried to hide the toilet paper, they found it. He stacked it up high on nails, or sealed it in coffee cans or dangled from string inside the lid, but the crafty little squirrels found it, shredded it into neat piles of puffy mess and used it for their winter nesting material.

It became a comical battle of wits between George and those ingenious little creatures. I secretly rooted for the squirrels each time they thwarted George's efforts to keep them from nesting in the outhouse.

On the very last day of our final visit to the cabin, I left a twelve-roll package behind the door and wished them well as I spotted them chattering and darting from branch to branch in the trees above. I walked away smiling. I applauded their tenacity and hoped they would survive to pester the next owners.

A friendly cabin visitor

Taxi anyone?

20 LIKE DUCKS ON WATER

The following summer the boat was undergoing repairs. We were feeling landlocked and grumpy, unable to get out on the water. George and I sat in the truck parked close to the new floatplane dock built on Near Island a couple of years before. This location alleviated some of the noisy small plane traffic buzzing around Island Lake and the tiny Municipal runway. The bridge to Near Island, constructed in 1986, supported a much needed second boat harbor for the almost 700 ships that fished in the area, as well as the new floatplane dock.

We watched as a small-engine plane droned louder and louder as it dropped down from the sky, skied across the water through the channel. The floats spewed up watery foam in their wake, rippling outward, bouncing a family of ducks on the waves. The plane motored around to the dock and tied up to heavy metal cleats like a boat.

Seaplanes were a routine mode of transportation for people living on remote sites. The sleek little planes landed on lakes, lagoons and shallow bays picking up passengers, and delivering mail and supplies. They traveled to places where no runways, flat beaches, or landmasses were available that could accommodate wheeled planes. Seaplanes allowed access to the more remote parts of the island and the only other option besides a boat. Quicker, too.

We could get to our cabin in twelve minutes by floatplane, George explained one fall morning as he hung up the phone after confirming reservations for the next day. I shuddered with fright. It was one thing to stand on solid ground and watch one zoom in and zoom out, splashing up water and lifting off like carefree birds. It was totally different being one of those sick-looking passengers crawling in and out, at the hands of those death-defying pilots.

George was too excited to worry about such things. He seemed to take on new things with ease and eager anticipation, where I still struggled and stressed out and balked at attempting the unknown. Just as I would become accustomed to a new experience, up jumped something else to scare me. George would push and pull me gently along, feet dragging, head shaking, my mind and body protesting in quivering quakes.

Later, I was grateful for these experiences, glad that I had accomplished each new adventure, happy and content again with my newfound courage and resilience. But it was the getting there that concerned me. And this journey was way beyond my comfort zone.

I sat next to George stuffed into my seat with my knees bent up almost touching my chest, the metal side of the tiny plane smashed cold against my shoulder. George looked around the plane with his usual curiosity as the pilot went through his checklist.

I trembled uncontrollably and squeezed George's hand to numbness as we bounced on the waves, lifted off just above the water, and climbed slowly up into the sky. Panic rose with the plane, higher and higher as I watched the wake below, foamy and rippling away on both sides, sending the waves quickly to shore and back.

We had left no tracks, no trace, and no way to follow our trail. We were flying now, to somewhere else inaccessible: our cabin. We bounced and bobbed through the air like a bumblebee, barely a hundred feet from green grassy hillsides. The miniature plane slipped between mountain peaks, curved around valleys and suddenly dropped terrifying close to steep ravines, and finally drifted over the sparkling blue ocean again. The pilot eased back the engine and we slowed to almost a hover above the waves then dropped down on the water with a slight bump. The floatplane skied across the waves like a duck on a pond.

The jovial pilot cut the engine and we rode the wake to shore, the bottom of the floats sliding up onto the gritty beach and slowing the metal bottom to a stop as the tail bounced slightly with the waves rolling to shore. The pilot opened his tiny door and deftly stepped down, balancing neatly on the top of the float and opened the door next to George.

George stepped down easily onto the float, reached for his backpack, and then for my hand. I latched on to him with one arm, reached for my backpack and tumbled out of the plane as my foot caught on the ledge. George steadied me upright, countering my forward lean, and then stepped off the float onto the beach, tugging me along behind him. The courteous pilot said nothing, but I caught a small grin on his face before he turned to fiddle with the door latch on the plane.

"Thanks, Willy," George said, shaking hands with the friendly pilot.

"See you two in a week," Willy reminded as he shoved the plane easily off the sand and hopped back on to the float. "Same beach, one hour earlier to catch the high tide, okay?"

"Right. We'll be here," George said.

"Need anything, call us on six six."

"Got it," George replied, snapping his hand to his forehead in a merry salute. VHF radio had several channels; the only two I knew were sixteen, for emergencies, and the one the locals used, six six. VHF radio was the only communication available at the time on boats and especially at remote locations. This severe inconvenience always made me a little nervous. While I had all the confidence in George's ability to figure things out, fix anything broken, or rig up anything that would work even temporarily, what if something happened to George? What would I do? How would I be able to manage? I could not push these nagging thoughts away as I stood on that now familiar but faraway beach.

Cold chills clutched my chest as Willy hopped back in the plane, started the engine and drifted back out into the ocean. The only means of getting off this island was floating away, puttering, turning, gaining speed, skiing out past the waves, lifting up, up, up. Off the water and into the sky the small but extremely useful airplane flew away, the waves from the wake rippling out and back over the sand where we stood. Alone.

In less than thirty seconds, there was no trace of him. There were no dents in the sand where the floats sat, and no foot tracks from Willy. The waves had scrubbed the beach clean in the next instant. The water seeped up the sand and fell back into the ocean, whipping away all signs of activity.

For a moment I felt a panic, a burning desire to run, wave back the plane, shout and wave and cry, "Wait, don't leave us here, come back, come back!" I saw George out of the corner of my eye raise his arm too. *He felt the same way,* I thought. *He was panicked, too.* But no. George's arm teetered back and forth slowly, waving and smiling at the pilot. Not frantically, like I wanted to do.

I put my arm up too, clutched it with my other hand and willed it to sway slowly, side to side, in time with George's arm. The pilot waved back, tipping shiny wings slightly right then left then straight again as he drifted farther away. We watched in silence until the bright orange plane disappeared on the other side of the mountain and the engine hummed out of hearing.

George turned to me. He wore a small smile, his blue eyes bright with barely contained excitement. A look I immediately responded to—most times not knowing what to expect—but his enthusiasm was always contagious and it always lightened my mood. I gazed back at him, fear and anxiety slipping away, washing out with the receding waves. I suddenly felt a new excitement as I studied his face.

I slowly began to understand George's communication. There we were, completely alone and marooned on an island. Everybody's dream-come-true. No people, no phones, no television - just nature and us. The wildlife swirled all around us. Elegant eagles soared overhead, silly seagulls squawked at one another, ducks drifted on top of rounded waves, and sea otters floated on their backs in the distance, clack, clack, clacking their clamshells against a rock.

We stood still for a few moments longer, listening to the sweet sounds of wilderness. We gazed at the artistic vista of green mountains, snow-capped with silver slivers of waterfalls climbing down crevices, cascading over rocks, slicing down through green grass, alders, and spruce trees, and leaving chocolate edges on the sides of the streaming water. We tasted the tangy salt spray stuck to our faces in tiny specks of white dots and inhaled the fresh tangy air of damp sand and musty moss.

The summer sun was high in the sky although it was nearly 4 p.m. In our dreamlike happiness, we felt the success of achieving one thing in life, the thing that seemed so distant, so unreachable. But there we were. George and I became fully aware of what we had. This was it. This was what we had dreamed of for so long. Of course, there were no palm trees, no sweltering tropical breeze, and no waiters about, but this was better, different. Not the ordinary dream, not the island in our minds we pictured so long ago, but a different island—green with lush vegetation, sparkling azure water, and soft sandy beaches. We didn't have umbrella drinks, but we had bottled water. George and I bumped the bottles together, lifted them towards the sea, and took two long gulps.

The light breeze felt warm on my face. It was an unusual 69 degrees on this lovely day. We hoisted on our backpacks, hiked up the beach, through the woods on the well-worn animal trail, opened the door to the cabin, and stopped still.

Someone had been there. Not recently, but within the last two months. Human, not animal, as we had sometimes thought we would find. An empty telltale wrapper from a dried soup mix layed on the floor, and a carton of Sprite was opened with four cans missing. Initially, we were shocked. It felt like an invasion. Neither of us had given anyone permission to use the cabin while we were gone.

George snatched up the wrapper and tossed it in the bucket in the corner then quickly scanned the rest of the spaces. I followed his eyes to the woodstove. There on the left side was a neat little pile of sticks and kindling stacked about three feet by two. Whoever stayed here had helped themselves to our provisions but they left a nice pile of wood in return.

I had begun to feel bad for jumping to conclusions. My feelings changed from annoyance to almost acceptance of the intruder, even to wonderment about whether he or they were okay. Perhaps they had been caught in a storm and took refuge there, in which case, we were happy to oblige. I wished, however, that they had at least left a note.

After that first time, we occasionally found the cabin such, and never pursued or bothered to find out who the uninvited guests were. We stuck to our belief that someone needed it and usually they left some token of appreciation behind. No damage had been done, no harm came to any items, and so we became accustomed to it. After all, when a storm struck, it was best to seek shelter in a hurry. In that case, we were glad they had found our place and maintained a certain respect for our cabin, as well.

21 FISHING FOR BEAR

It was another summer weekend when we once again motored out to our cabin, looking forward to relaxing in quiet
solitude. We spent an entertaining evening listening to songbirds
tweeting and the occasional splashing and clacking of otters
playing close to shore. George grilled steaks and I kept the foiled
potatoes turning on the fire. We enjoyed our cozy campfire meal,
and then turned in for the night.

The next morning, however drizzly, brought calm waters
and an easy breeze so we decided to go fishing in the lagoon not
far from the cabin. George and I loaded our gear and launched
the skiff, paddling out past the reefs and rocks. Once clear of
any hidden obstacles, George switched the engine down into the
water, started it up and steered the boat around, heading along
the shoreline.

After a ten-minute cruise, we slipped into Litnik Bay and
up onto a sandy area. I jumped out and grabbed the bow, while
George cut the engine, switched the prop to the up position
and hopped out. Together we heaved the skiff farther up on the
beach. I unloaded the backpacks, tackle box and rods while
George pulled out the anchor rope and attached it to a heavy log.
The tide was going out, so we had about three hours to try our

luck. We walked single file along a well-worn trail that led into the woods for about 50 yards, and then came back out to a small clearing just past the mouth of the river.

"This'll do." George set the tackle box down on a grassy bank, fixed a lure to his rod and cast out into the fast-moving river. I took a few steps farther along the bank and cast out. A silver salmon jumped up from the water close to the bank on other side and splashed back down. A good sign. A steep cliff rose up on the opposite side of the river with pretty waterfalls that rumbled down and splashed onto large rounded rocks, sending sparkles of spray and half moon rainbows glistening above the river.

"Got 'em," George yelled, quickly reeling in the reluctant fish. He caught the first one and then the second, while I kept getting my line snagged on underwater rocks or overhanging tree branches. I had become frustrated as the minutes ticked by and George's stringer was filling up with fish. "Upbeat and positive" was George's nagging voice inside my head. I took a deep breath, exhaled slowly and cast out several more times.

Whomp! Finally, I hooked one. I tugged hard, reeled as fast as I could, and backed up on the bank. The fish tugged back and leaped out of the water. Jerking back and forth, reeling and running, I battled it out with the stubborn fish.

"I got one," I shouted in as calm a tone as I could muster, trying to keep a solemn composure like some pro. I cranked the handle on the reel and the line whizzed and squealed, the fish splashed and churned in the fast-moving river, and then darted in the opposite direction, zipping the line back off the reel. I fought with the drag and held tight to the rod as it jerked my arms wildly around. The fish changed course again as I frantically cranked the lever round and round as fast as I could. Whiz, crank, whiz, crank. I was making progress. The fish was giving up.

I was breathing hard as I pulled him up the wet, slippery bank, walking backwards as I focused on my prize. I reeled in the slack as I walked forward down to the river again, watching the fish flip-flop in the sand. I unhooked my stringer, ran one end through the gills, and clipped it shut. Ha! I had him at last. I was proud of my catch. I had broken my bad luck spell and caught a big fat fish. I had one, and now for another.

"There's a bear! Clare! Clare!" The waterfall drowned most of it out, but I did hear the last word George said from several yards downriver: *Clare*. I thought he was praising my hard-won effort and waved a hand without looking up as I clamped the fish stringer to my belt loop. George yelled again. I straightened up and there he was.

We had learned to listen carefully when we went into the woods. The sound of nature was beautiful. Sweet chirping birds, buzzing bees, swishing grasses blowing softly in the breeze, the rhythmic whooshing of the ocean gently rolling back and forth over the sandpaper sand. But I hadn't heard him. I had let my guard down.

The waterfalls had drowned out everything except the fun of catching the fish. I had focused on the splashing and leaping and plopping and finally the victory, as I hauled in my first catch of the day. Not that bears typically made much noise, but the other critters seemed to know the sounds-sometimes the forest grew quiet, too quickly, which usually meant a bear was nearby. No creature wanted to attract a bear's attention.

The large dark brown bear plodded down the same path we had used. Foolishly, I had glared at him with annoyance, think-ing he had followed us like some lonely lost dog. His head lolled slightly back and forth and his huge pan-size paws made puffs in the dirt as he sauntered towards us. The bear seemed unhurried, unafraid, and fortunately for us, unaware of us, for the moment.

George darted quickly over to me, snatched me by the shoul-der and shoved me up the bank towards the nearest tree.

"Climb the tree, Clare, climb the tree, now!" George ran to the next tree and jumped up, grabbing the lowest branch and scampering up with all the agility of a monkey. I was still on the ground, trying to reach up with my right hand to a branch, but the rod and stringer with my prize fish dangling at the other end was making it difficult to maneuver.

I tried frantically to tuck the rod inside my raincoat but the reel caught on the second button. It wouldn't go down any farther. I pushed and tugged and jerked it around, jamming this way and that but it wouldn't go. The weight of the fish on the stringer was jerking my other hand back and forth as it swung and bounced, throwing my aim off balance. I stomped from one foot to the other in my anxious state, twisting the rod around with one hand and keeping a worried eye on the fish swinging restlessly in the other. The rod still wouldn't go in any farther and I couldn't quite reach the branch, hanging just inches above my head. I glanced up at the branch, down at the fish, and then up again.

The bear sneezed behind me. Or snorted or huffed or snuffed or whatever bears did when they smelled food. He was, by then, only a few yards away from me.

"What are you doing, Clare? Get up the tree now!" shouted George from a branch at the top of another tree.

Fear and George's voice screaming through my cluttered nervous brain had finally overridden my resentment at losing my hard-won catch of the day. I dropped everything to the ground and leaped for the branch. I yanked myself up, clunked a boot into a knothole, and then reached up again, and again in a rapid, panicky motion. I pulled myself up, and then up again, driven by that urgent survival instinct. I climbed as high as I could get before the limbs got too thin to hold my weight, then stopped. With a death grip on the narrow tip of the tree trunk, I dared to look down.

Far below, the bear ambled over to the tree and made a bee-line for my fish. He sniffed the string line, decided it was harmless, and pressed one giant paw on the fish head. He chomped down on the middle, tearing away a large chunk of skin and flesh. Next he scraped out the entrails and chewed rapidly, strings of goo dripping from his jaws and streaks of red blood spattering around his chin. In another three chomps, the fish was gone and the bear raised his mammoth brown head. He peered hungrily up the tree. I froze. His eyes locked on me like laser beams; I felt the red pinpoints stop on my forehead. He swung his head back and forth and pawed the ground, evidently trying to decide whether I was worth the trouble of knocking down the tree. He sniffed the air once more and circled the tree. Cub bears climbed trees often, when danger was near, but a full-grown bear typically didn't bother. He was too big and too old to climb, or so I had hoped.

A splash turned his head toward the river. With another sniff and huff the bear turned to the river and sauntered down to the bank. He turned his head once back at the tree then waded into the river for easier pickings. George and I had waited a long time in those trees while the bear caught and ate no less than twelve large fish, and then sauntered back up the path and into the woods.

I heard scraping on tree bark and branches rustling as George clambered down the to the ground. He appeared under my tree peering up between the branches, just where the bear had been.

"It's okay, come on down now." He waved a hand downward.

By that time my arms were numb, I couldn't feel my feet in my boots, and couldn't figure out which appendage to move first. Fear had turned me into petrified wood. My body was not listening to my head. I knew I had to climb down, but didn't have the faintest clue how to go about it. My mind was as numb as my arms. I couldn't register any thoughts in a direction that would help. I was frozen in some time warp. The quiet nature and burbling river were lulling me along through space.

"Move Clare, before that bear comes back for a second helping."

I moved. Diversion works. Plus, the thought of being the bear's second helping jump-started my mind and body into gear in an instant. Like an automated flow chart, I pulled up with one hand, untangled my left foot, dropped it down to the next branch, then my right hand found another branch, then my right foot and so on. Eventually I was on the ground with only minor scrapes and scratches.

George grabbed the front of my jacket, pulling me towards him, and I started to wrap my arms around him when he deftly stuck his hand down inside, pulled out the snack pack that had clogged the passageway inside my jacket, let go of me and turned to get the tackle box. I stumbled forward, hugging space. I quickly swatted away my weak gesture, flinging my arms as if to ward of a swarm of mosquitoes when George turned back around. We gathered the remaining gear, hiked back to the boat, loaded up, and pushed off. We returned to the cabin without my prize fish, but fortunately, we had lived to try again another day.

George and I had enjoyed the times we spent at our remote hideaway cabin for many more years. We hosted local friends and visitors from faraway, had picnics on the beach and caught many fish. Sometimes we just relaxed on the deck, watching the tides come and go in the calming ebb and flow, refreshing our spirits, refreshing our souls.

22 DEPARTING

People chose to live in certain places for many reasons, be it jobs, family, environment or economics. George and I kept moving from place to place to improve our careers and find our ideal environment, but I had grown tired of the constant changes. When I arrived in Kodiak, I was determined to stay put, no matter what. I had no idea at the time, what that would entail.

I discovered that Kodiak was a place where the natural elements forced one to plan and prepare from one day to the other, one season to the next. The rain and wind and snow and cold had put me on a schedule that only Mother Nature permitted—or didn't. The cost of elbow room was high, but people who lived here rose to the challenge and found the rewards well worth it. There were days when we traveled to the end of the forty-mile road in either direction from the center of town and hadn't seen any other cars on the road. Or we floated out in the bay in our small humble boat, or sat on a beach, or walked in the woods in peaceful solitude. There were other times when we gathered with many friends and shared delightful stories about fishing and crabbing and bears.

There was a high price to pay for that unique opportunity to find our spirits and test our strength of character, but the quality

of life we found on Kodiak was priceless. It was rugged, difficult, majestic, cold, windy and rainy, and sometimes sunny with
long hours of daylight followed by angry dark clouds and long
hours of darkness.

I became aware with mind and body of the value of my surroundings and the knowledge and strength I had gained from
that tough-love teacher, Mother Nature.

But alas, it was time once again for us to move on.

The orange ball of sun had slipped halfway behind the
rounded top of the mountain, casting a rich autumn glow of
golden light across the fading green hillside. Streaks of pink and
purple painted the sky and reflected softly in the ripples of the
blue sea below. It was our last night on this quiet beautiful island
and we were savoring every moment.

Over the past two years, George and I had begun to discuss
the next phase of our lives. We had both retired, and the high
cost of living on the island would no longer be affordable. We
could have stayed, of course, by cutting back to bare bones on
some things, but that was not what we wanted. It would have
meant we could no longer participate in the various activities we
had so loved in the early days.

There were other things to consider, like the long dark winters and decreasing physical fitness that limited the ability to
maintain the lifestyle we had become accustomed to. When we
were young, we seemed to barely notice as we busied ourselves
with brisk wintry activities of cross-country skiing, ice fishing,
and long walks with our beloved dogs on silent moonlit nights,
and the pleasurable but vigorous activities of fishing and hunting, pulling crab pots and picking gillnets. We were getting older
as the cycle of life would have it, which meant we needed to
switch gears to a less strenuous lifestyle.

George made one last attempt to ease the pain of our dreaded
but necessary departure. He turned to me in time to see the tiny
tear slide down my cheek that I hadn't bothered to hide.

"It'll be okay, Clare, you'll see. It's all good, right? Besides," he said in his quiet, soothing tone, "we need to let some other young couple have a turn, now, right? It's their chance to enjoy some elbow room."

In my mind's eye, I took one last turn atop Pillar Mountain. I twirled in a slow circle, arms stretched out from my sides, face upturned, soaking in the panoramic view of the vast blue ocean reaching out to the crescent-shaped horizon. I saw the soft green manicured mountains of fuzzy lichen, alders, and stately spruce trees protruding upwards, dividing ocean from sky, sporting their ever-present snow caps. The salty bull kelp breeze filled my nose, mingled with a sweet mixture of wild blue lupines, tiny white blossoms of clover and brown-lipped lilies scattered along the grassy slopes. The quiet calming spirit of nature and the vast open wilderness filled me once again with its essence of serenity.

But George was right, as he was on most occasions - it was time to leave. The house was sold, along with all of its contents, as well as the old reliable Dodge truck that had served us well on slippery roads and the snow-drifted driveway through the years. The sturdy Bobcat, our mechanical workhorse, went to a friend for continued use and the four-wheelers had been sold for a good price.

Everything was tied up in a neat package of finality. There was nothing left to do but drive down to the ferry terminal. George sat behind the wheel of our small SUV and steered to the directions of the ship's crewmember, who rapidly swung his arms this way and that, guiding us into the enormous depths of the cargo area of the Tustumena.

Finally wedged into a tight place surrounded by several other cars, trucks, and heavy equipment, we left the car and climbed up to the deck as the ship blew the mournful whistle announcing departure. The thick ropes were untied and flung over to the waiting men, caught and stashed in their places. The engines roared to life and water churned underneath the giant ship as we stood on the deck and waved goodbye to our longtime friends whom we knew would stay on and continue the challenge.

Pete was there in the crowd, old and wrinkled now, and a little stooped from his logging labor, along with our cabin builders, Cole and Lenny, their faces long and tired but still wearing their lopsided grins, and there was silly Matt, still skipping carelessly through life albeit somewhat slower. We smiled at our rugged fishermen friends and their steadfast wives, and the strong-willed ladies of the Far North, who had kept me motivated through the tough times.

I had noted others who were absent from the group and missed them terribly, like Jerry, who had long since moved to Montana, and Walter, who had returned home to Mississippi, and of course Tom and his lovely wife, and old Carl, who were no longer of this world.

The ship drifted slowly away from the dock, the huge propellers shoving back the water in deep swirls and foam. I held onto the rail, as tight as I could, knowing that if I let go, I would have jumped for shore. George sensed my pain and put his arm around me. I leaned into him, and thus we stood as the ship slipped slowly past the familiar sights along the shore of canneries, restaurants, the local power company, and the colorful houses clinging to the gray rocky cliffs and grassy hillsides. We slumbered past tiny fishing boats and waved as the friendly people waved back.

We stood together, side by side, reliving one last time the magic and mysterious spirit of nature we had found, the visions of our Kodiak life flashed by like a slideshow until we could no longer see the island.

George opened my hand and sprinkled a small amount of black sand from a paper cup into my palm. It was moist and smelled of kelp, fish, and salt water. I gazed at the small mound through blurry, tear-filled eyes as he poured another pile into his own hand. We faced each other, locked into the shared moment, and stretched out our arms over the rail.

"On the count of three, we let go." George held my eyes as I slowly nodded. We counted together quietly as we leaned over the railing, all four hands gripped tightly together. On three we loosened our grips and the sand dribbled too quickly through our fingers, falling into the sea. We had physically and symbolically left our island behind.

After a few moments of silence, George suddenly nudged me in the ribs with his elbow. "Come on, let's go plan our next adventure!"

9 781593 307493